The Hebrew Academy of Cleveland

*F*ounded in 1943, the Hebrew Academy of Cleveland is a nationally acclaimed institution educating over 750 children. Its scope encompasses more than transmitting knowledge and inculcating Jewish culture. Our obligation is to continue the glorious chain of our Mesorah and develop a love for Torah, Am Yisrael and Eretz Yisrael.

The growth of the Hebrew Academy — from a basement classroom with a handful of students, to today's magnificent complex with a record enrollment — has been remarkable.

Educational aids and curriculum materials prepared at the Academy are implemented in day schools nationally and across the globe.

The Academy today offers a complete religious and secular educational program from pre-kindergarten through the Philip and Mary Edlis Elementary School, the Jacob Sapirstein Mesivta High School for Boys and the Beatrice Stone Yavne High School for Girls.

Education is provided in a wholesome environment fostering moral and ethical behavior in the Torah-true tradition. Education never stops at the Academy. From early morning Mishnayos class to Voluntary After-School programs, Torah study thrives. Extracurricular projects and recreational activities help foster leadership skills and enhance the students' spirit of Torah.

Another Academy innovation is the Summer Torah Enrichment Program. Camp S.T.E.P. — as it is called — is a full-scale Torah and activities program offering its campers 2½ hours of intensive learning each morning, followed by swimming, sports, and exciting trips. A separate Yavne girls Camp S.T.E.P. has developed into a full six-week program, as the Academy continues to serve the community.

The latest addition has been a separate division for 75 immigrant children. Special classes and tutors have been provided to enable them to learn and grow as Torah Jews.

Over 5,000 students have been educated at the Academy, many of whom have assumed leadership positions across the globe. *Indeed, the Jewish leaders of tomorrow are in the Academy classrooms today.*

פנינים
הגדה
של פסח

A Publication of the
Hebrew Academy of Cleveland

The Peninim
HAGGADAH

*Haggadah Text
with English Translation;
Thought-Provoking Insights
and An Informative Question & Answer Section*

by Rabbi A.L. Scheinbaum

The Peninim Haggadah

ISBN: 0-9635120-7-2

Published and distributed by:
Peninim Publications in conjunction with
The Hebrew Academy of Cleveland
1860 S. Taylor Road, Cleveland Hts., Ohio 44118
216-321-5838 Ext 165
Fax: 216-321-0588

Cover design & page layout:
Bottom Line Design/Brooklyn, NY.
718-332-8134

Printed in the United States of America

Cover Photo:
Courtesy of American Greetings Corp.

עטרת זקנים בני בנים ותפארת בנים אבותם
(משלי יז, ו)

"The crown of the aged are their children's children,
and the glory of children are their parents."
(Mishlei 17:6)

Dedicated by

Sidney and Phyllis Reisman

**In honor of our children
and grandchildren**

Mrs. Ramie Resnick
Jordan and Illyssa

Jeffrey and Lori Schwartz
Sean, Kayla, Brandon and Brooke

Dr. Tony and Wendy Reisman
Danielle

Peter Reisman

**Dedicated in loving memory of our dear
Parents and Grandparents**

Nathan and Gertrude Lippe

A quiet and unassuming man, Dad taught by example. His sterling character was an inspiration to all those who were privileged to know him.

Mom's abundant love and selfless devotion to her family will always be cherished. Her warm smile and good nature will be missed.

With everlasting love,

Gary & Randi Lippe
Brooke, Danielle & Jordan

Dedicated by
Andrew and Pamela Farkas

In loving memory of our Grandmother

Ambassador Ruth Farkas

"A woman of integrity and valor"

אשת חיל מי ימצא ורחוק מפנינים מכרה
(משלי לא, י)

"A woman of valor who can find,
far beyond pearls is her value."

(Mishlei 31:10)

למזכרת נצח בהיכל הספר

לז"נ אבי מורי

ר' נח ב"ר יהודה אריה שיינבוים ז"ל

נפטר כ"ב כסלו תשכ"ו

לז"נ מר חמי

ר' שלמה זלמן ב"ר יצחק בריננער ז"ל

נפטר ב' דר"ח אייר תשכ"ח

לז"נ אחיותי שנקטפו בילדותן ע"י הנאצים הארורים ימ"ש

רחל לאה ע"ה

פריידא ע"ה

שרה אסתר ע"ה

שיינבוים

נשמתן עלו בטהרה י"ג תשרי תש"ב

מרדכי גיפטער
ישיבת טלז
Rabbi Mordecai Gifter
28570 Nutwood Lane
Wickliffe, Ohio 44092

בעז״ה

ב׳ אדר א׳ התשנ״ז

לכבוד יקירי הרב ר׳ אברהם לייב שיינבוים נר״ו

לאחדשה״ט

באתי בזה לברך את יקירי ר׳ אברהם לייב נר״ו לכבוד
הוצאת פרי עבודתו לכבוד חג הפסח ״הגדה של פסח״.
מטעם חולשתי אי אפשר לי לעבור על מאמריך, אולם
כבר אתחזק בפרי עבודתו להוציא דבר נאה ומתוקן אשר
יש בהם רב תועלת למלמדים בבתי ספר חרדיים לקרב
לב ישראל לאביהם שבשמים.

יהא ה׳ בעזרו להפיץ מעיינותיו חוצה, ויזכה לרוות רב
נחת וברכה מכל יו״ח.

באהבה

Beatrice J. Stone, Yavne High School • Hebrew Academy of Cleveland   Jacob Sapirstein Mesivta High School

בית חנוך עברי דקליבלנד
Hebrew Academy of Cleveland
1860 SOUTH TAYLOR ROAD • CLEVELAND, OHIO 44118 • (216) 321-5838

טו' בשבט תשנ"ז

הנה כבר איתמחי גברא המחנך הותיק הרה"ג ר' אברהם ליב שייננוים
שליט"א הנודע בשערים עם הדפסת פנינים על פרשיות השבוע שזכה להפצה
מרובה בכל רחבי תבל, ועכשיו עלה במחשבתו לסדר ולהדפיס פנינים על הגדה
של פסח.

יברכהו השי"ת ויזכה גם בזה לברך על המוגמר להדפיס ולהפיץ על
ההגדה מעיינות רבותינו ז"ל שמפיהם אנו חיים ומימיהם אנו שותים להגדיל
תורה ולהאדירה.

נחום זאב דסלר

TORAH UMESORAH
תורה ומסורה

The National Society
for Hebrew Day Schools

COMMITTING
GENERATIONS
TO TORAH

6 Shevat 5757
January 14, 1997

It is a pleasure and privilege to share my enthusiasm about Rabbi A. Leib
Scheinbaum's Peninim Haggadah. His Peninim series on Parshas Hashavua
has graced countless Shabbos tables, inspiring many families with profound
Torah thoughts and stories.

I am thrilled to see that Rabbi Scheinbaum's newest treasure, the Peninim
Haggadah, will now be available to enhance the quintessential Jewish
educational experience, the Pesach Seder. With it's thought-provoking essays
and dynamic question-answer format, the Peninim Haggadah will be a most
welcome and valuable companion to the family seder for generations to come.

Sincerely yours,

Rabbi Joshua Fishman
Executive Vice-President

160 BROADWAY, 4th Fl.

NEW YORK, NY 10038

TEL: (212) 227-1000

FAX: (212) 406-6934

E-mail: umesorah @ aol.com

Table of Contents

Questions & Answers 87

Haggadah with English Translation ....
.... *Open from other side*

Preface

Each Jewish festival serves as a vehicle to teach fundamental lessons in our relationship with Hashem. *Pesach*, the Festival of Freedom is no different. Its message is both of a personal and national significance. Indeed, the chapter of Jewish history that addresses the servitude and liberation from Egypt is so profound and inscrutable that it must be studied over and over again. It is truly a study in itself. *"Zeicher Yetzias Mitzrayim"*, a remembrance of the exodus from Egypt, brings to mind more than a miraculous event in our history; it is the foundation upon which much of Jewish doctrine is based. It proclaims our nationhood. It is the key to understanding *gadlus Ha'boreh*, the greatness of Hashem the Creator. The spirit of our people is revived as we study the lessons of *Yetzias Mitzrayim*. We learn about Hashem's ways; His characteristics, His conduct, His mercy and His retributions.

The *Haggadah* is the primer from which we annually study the lessons of the Exodus. It guides and inspires as it relates the greatness of Hashem. We are filled with pride as we leaf through its pages, reading, studying and reflecting upon that unparalleled event. Each commentary adds a new perspective, a new dimension into the understanding of the occurrences and their message.

We have attempted to present a broad-based anthology of homilies and insights on the *Haggadah*. The concepts presented include expositions which are culled from and based upon the thoughts of our *Torah* luminaries of the past and present. They reflect authentic *Torah* perspectives on life. In keeping with the spirit of the *Yom Tov* we have included a section of review questions and answers on the topic of *Pesach*. We hope that this volume will inspire its readers, affording them the opportunity for personal development and educational enrichment through *Torah* study. We pray to Hashem that through these efforts we will merit the final redemption with the advent of *Moshiach Tzidkeinu*.

Avraham Leib Scheinbaum
Adar I 5757
Cleveland Hts, Ohio

Acknowledgments

It is very easy to delude oneself into thinking that the moderate success that he has achieved is his own. While my name appears on the cover, this work would never have reached fruition without the dedication and hard work of a number of people. They truly deserve the plaudits.

The *Hebrew Academy of Cleveland,* has been my "home" for the last seventeen years. *Rabbi N.W. Dessler, shlita,* its Dean, has been a mentor and friend during most of my endeavors in the field of *Torah chinuch.* His concern, interest and guidance have been major factors in my success. It was *Morry Weiss* who first encouraged my venture into publication. I will always be indebted to him for his support.

Gratitude, however, goes back further. Indeed, one can never fulfill the requirement to acknowledge and appreciate the gratitude owed to parents and mentors. My father, *Reb Noach Scheinbaum, z.l.,* was a man of sterling character whose uncompromising integrity inspired all who knew him. Together with my mother, *Mrs. Glika Bogen,* he labored with love to ensure his children a genuine *Torah* education. May she, together with her husband, *Mr. Simcha Bogen,* enjoy health, longevity, and *nachas* from their families. My father-in-law, *Reb Shlomo Zalman Brunner, z.l.,* was a man whose entire life was a lesson in the *middah* of *chesed.* Together with my mother-in-law, *Mrs. Feige Feldman,* they imparted a legacy of *ahavas Yisrael* and *ahavas chesed* to their children. May she and her husband, *Mr. Moshe Leib Feldman,* be blessed with health, longevity and *nachas.*

I owe an eternal debt of gratitude to that great citadel of *Torah,* the *Telshe Yeshiva,* and to its *Roshei Ha'Yeshiva, shlita,* for all the years I spent there studying *Torah.* I would especially like to single out my two *rebbeim* who are no longer with us, *Hagaon Horav Chaim Mordechai Katz, z.l.,* and *Hagaon Horav Rafael Boruch Sorotzkin, z.l.* Their lives epitomized *gadlus ba'Torah.*

No successful project is accomplished by a single individual. To this end I feel it incumbent to recognize those individuals who gave of themselves to see to it that this project reach successful fruition. The task of preparing the original manuscript was assumed by *Henny Dessler.* She exemplified patience and understanding throughout this endeavor. Her devotion and commitment to this project has been a major factor in its success. *Mrs. Marilyn Berger,* who carefully edited the text, has once again demonstrated her uncanny ability for enhancing the written word. Thanks to *Rabbi J. Hillel Yarmove,* who reviewed the questions and answers. *Mrs. Ethel Gottlieb* proofread and copyedited the entire manuscript. Her suggestions were valuable. *Mrs. Tova Scheinerman* and *Mrs. Chantal Modes* prepared the final copy.

Rabbi Malkiel Hefter is that bonding agent who keeps everything together. He spent countless hours assisting in the technical conception of this work. He is always there willing to help. *Yitzchok Saftlas* and *Yaakov Gerber* of *Bottom Line Design* labored strenuously to produce a *sefer* that is aesthetically appealing. Their endeavor adds the crowning touch to this project.

The reinforcement and support of my family have always been the driving forces behind my work. My children have accepted an absentee father and have given me the moral support and stimulus to pursue this endeavor.

Last, but not least, I pay tribute to my wife, מנב"ת *Neny.* She helped me to continue my studies for many years after our marriage and willingly shares in my *harbotzas Torah,* wherever it may be. She has been a tower of strength and an unfailing source of encouragement without whom this work would never have been completed. She sacrifices much, often assuming the role of mother and father, so that I may pursue my work. Her valor as a woman and forbearance as a wife have proven to be instructive to our children and an inspiration to me. May we, together with our children, merit that the love of *Torah,* its study and dissemination, be the hallmarks of our home.

Avraham Leib Scheinbaum
Rosh Chodesh Adar 1 5757
Cleveland Heights, Ohio

פנינים הגדה של פסח
The Peninim
HAGGADAH

Insights
Section

The *Seder – Order or Confusion?*

Seder means order. It implies a predictable pattern, an ordered sequence. Consequently, we would expect total order on the night of *Pesach*, the night when we recount the whole story of *Pesach* from the origin of slavery to the ultimate liberation. To the contrary, the events of the night of *Pesach* are not presented in an orderly fashion. We read about the deaths of an entire nation's first-born; the escape of slaves from a country that was previously considered escape proof; oppressors presenting their freeing slaves with gifts. This was a night that was as bright as day! Does this scenario indicate order, or does it suggest chaos?

The *Sfas Emes* distinguishes between the natural world, a world of orderly laws, and the supernatural world, the world in which the natural order is suspended and miracles reign. In the natural world, the rising and setting of the sun is but one of the many thousands of predictable events that follow a pre-established pattern. In the world of miracles, the spiritual world, there is no set order. The *Maharal* explains that in the natural world the pattern of occurrences follows a cause and effect relationship. When one throws a stick down it lands on the ground. In the miraculous world, we never know what to expect. The will of Hashem dominates. [This does not mean that the will of Hashem does not determine events in the physical world. It is just that in the physical world Hashem's will is that life follow a certain pattern.] In the miraculous world, when Moshe throws down a stick, it is transformed into a snake. In the physical world, when one walks into the Red Sea, he gets wet and eventually drowns. In the miraculous world, the sea splits and the people walk through, dry and comfortable. Hashem conducts *Bnei Yisrael's* lives with miracles. Cause and effect do not necessarily apply to His people, because Hashem does what He desires for us.

True, *Pesach* night commemorates the "unpredictable" – because that is actually what we have come to expect. *Bnei Yisrael* had not yet achieved that spiritual level where they would merit this miraculous order. Time was passing however, and were they to remain in Egypt, they would be risking spiritual extinction. Hashem took them out of the physical realm of material objects and enabled them to rush out of Egypt. The *Sfas Emes* makes an analogy which elucidates this point. The royal prince once brought a beggar into the palace kitchen so that the royal chef would feed them both. Out of fear of being caught feeding the beggar, the chef quickly fed him and chased him from the kitchen. The prince continued to stay on even after the beggar left. One of the kitchen staff questioned the cook; "Why does the prince remain and not the beggar?" The chef responded, "The beggar is lucky that I did not strike him as soon as he walked through the door. The prince, on the other hand, can do what he wants. After all, he is the king's son."

Likewise, when *Bnei Yisrael* were about to leave Egypt they had to be rushed. They had not yet attained the level of the "king's son." This is a level to which we aspire, when *Moshiach* will come. On *Pesach* night, things change. We are not in exile; it is the night of our liberation! On this night, we recall the series of miraculous events to which we only allude during the year. Tonight we talk about *geulah,* redemption. We discuss the *geulah* that occurred in Egypt, as well as the one that we anticipate with the advent of *Moshiach*, when the miraculous order will be permanently "natural.

Freedom – How Rich We Really Are!

*O*ne of the significant rituals which express the idea of *cheirus*, freedom, is the drinking of the four cups of wine. Indeed, *halachah* demands that even a poor man must drink the four *kosos*, cups of wine, even if he must go from door to door, begging for money to buy wine. Throughout Jewish law, we find that it's far better to forego performing a *mitzvah* than to destroy one's dignity and self-esteem. Yet, when it comes to the four cups of wine, we are adjured to beg in order to avail ourselves the wherewithal to purchase wine.

Imagine a person who throughout the rest of the year suffices with whatever he can scrape together. On *Shabbos* he eats a simple meal without the special *Shabbos* extras. His *Shabbos* wardrobe is extremely limited. When it comes to *Pesach*, however, he must resort to going from door to door seeking the pennies that will provide him with the *arba kosos*. Why? So, that he can sit back at the *Seder* and feel like a free man. But what free man has to go from door to door begging for wine? Is this the nature of freedom?

Horav Moshe Schwab, z"l, explains that the *Torah's* idea of freedom is unlike ours. A free man is one who is liberated from the shackles of the *yetzer hora*, evil inclination. He is not swayed by its blandishments; he does not capitulate to its constant demands. Indeed, a free man is one who is in control. One may be wealthy but subservient to his desires. On the other hand, one may be relegated to standing on the street corner begging for alms and, yet, be considered emancipated. The key is an individual's ability to perform contrary to his physical desires, to be able to act in accordance with ultimate right, not his cravings. The more one is subjected to the whims of his desires, the greater the level of his indenture. One who has a million dollars, yet yearns for another million, is actually a poor man in regard to that second million. The wealthy man who is obsessed with satisfying his whims is, unfortunately, an unhappy servant to his *yetzer hora*. Is there really a poorer man than he?

Conversely, the poor man who takes great pride in his *avodas* Hashem, service to Hashem, who exalts in going from door to door begging to perform Hashem's command, is truly a *ben chorin*, free man. The lesson of this *halachah* is profound. The concept of freedom on *Pesach* is unlike the mundane idea of freedom. Every individual, according to his own nature and passions, is able to liberate himself from his personal servitude. He must understand the meaning of slavery before he can relate to freedom.

Reliving the Exodus

מה נשתנה הלילה הזה מכל הלילות? עבדים היינו לפרעה במצרים...
ויוציאנו ד' אלוקינו משם... ואילו לא הוציא הקב"ה את אבותינו
ממצרים הרי אנו ובנינו ובני בנינו משעבדים היינו לפרעה במצרים

Why is this night different from all the other nights? We were slaves to Pharaoh in Egypt but Hashem, our God, took us out of there...

Had not the Holy One Blessed is He taken our fathers out from Egypt, then we, our children and grandchildren would still be enslaved to Pharaoh in Egypt.

We have before us the underlying motif of the *Seder* night: "Why is this night different?" That is the fundamental question. One particular aspect of the distinction is not emphasized. *Horav Nissan Alpert, z"l,* explains the question in a noteworthy manner. When we think about it, *Pesach* is different from the other festivals and from *Shabbos* in one significant area, the food that we eat. During the rest of the year no specific diet must be observed. We have neither a special way to eat the food nor a special time frame during which it must be eaten. *Pesach* night, however, we are enjoined to eat certain foods that recall the exile and the exodus from Egypt.

We must recline when we eat, and we must finish before *chatzos*, midnight. Indeed, there is a detailed menu for the evening. What makes it more enigmatic is the conceptual basis of this menu. For instance, if a couple were to celebrate the anniversary of their wedding they would attempt to do something or eat a food that evokes that special event. No one would plan a huge celebration each year to commemorate a wedding! On *Pesach* night we are doing more than merely celebrating the original Exodus; we are actually reliving it!

That essentially, claims *Horav* Alpert, is the response to the *Mah Nishtanah*. The *Seder* night is not just a mere commemoration of the Exodus, it is actually reliving the Exodus! If Hashem had not liberated our ancestors from Egypt, then we would still be there today! The redemption was for *our* sake. Our ancestors could have really waited a bit longer. After all, the individuals who had deviated from Judaism were gone, and those who remained devoted could have waited until it was the appropriate time for redemption. Hashem "hurried" the redemption in order to save the next generation of children that would be born into the decadence of Egypt.

We celebrate *Yetzias Mitzrayim* on *Pesach* because it was for us. We do not simply remember the Exodus, we relive it. We are playing an active role in the redemption, because we are experiencing it every *Pesach*. We are not merely celebrating the anniversary; we are metaphorically attending the *chasunah*!

A Process With Purpose

עבדים היינו לפרעה במצרים ויוציאנו ד' אלוקינו משם ביד חזקה
ובזרוע נטויה

We were slaves to Pharaoh in Egypt, but Hashem our God took us out
from there with a mighty hand and an outstretched arm.

hy were the Jews compelled to be slaves to Pharaoh? Indeed, why during the *Bris bein Ha'besarim* was it decreed
that *Bnei Yisrael* would be persecuted for four hundred years in Egypt?
Finally, what is the meaning of the phrase, "*And afterwards they shall
leave with great wealth?*" (This prophesy was delivered to Avraham at
the same time that the decree of "four hundred years" of slavery was
issued.) What does this great wealth consist of? It cannot be a reference to material wealth, for money can never adequately reimburse us
for the inhuman torture to which we were subjected for so many years.

The *Alshich Ha'Kadosh* explains that the purpose of *galus Mitzrayim*
was to purify and cleanse *Klal Yisrael*, so that they would be able to
assume a position of *kedushah* appropriate for receiving the *Torah*. Egypt
is likened to a crucible used to melt unrefined gold. After it is heated,
the worthless matter is separated, and the pure gold remains. The persecution and suffering endured by the Jews in Egypt freed them from
their spiritual impurities, so that when they left they were free of any
blemishes. They were truly prepared for *Kabbolas Ha'Torah*.

This purification process did not happen suddenly. The first par-
ticipant was Avraham *Avinu*. Hashem tested him ten times, and he
emerged triumphant. Yitzchak was destined to be the *olah temimah*,
pure, unblemished sacrifice. His level of *kedushah* was to be exemplary. Yishmael preceded him in birth and, therefore, absorbed
whatever spiritual blemishes might have resulted from Avraham's
yetzer hora. Yitzchak was born to parents who were both aged.
Avraham *Avinu* was one hundred years old, much past his prime. His
yetzer hora, however limited, no longer existed. Sarah *Imeinu* was
considerably beyond the age of childbearing. Thus, while Yitzchak's
birth was miraculous, we know he was also very pure in pedigree.
Eisav's birth preceded Yaaakov's and forged the way for his brother
by absorbing any of the spiritual impurities.

Bnei Yisrael, Yaakov *Avinu's* descendants, went down to Egypt. They were tortured, but they prevailed over their adversaries. Not all of the Jews were perfect. Four- fifths perished during the three days of darkness. Those who were privileged to leave – who were worthy of the Exodus – had undergone the purification process, and were prepared to advance further. This is the meaning of, *"And afterwards they will leave with great wealth."* The transformation of the Jew, was in fact the real treasure. The *Torah* does not say, "רכוש רב" *much* wealth; rather, it, says "רכוש גדול" great wealth, a reference to the spiritual wealth of which they had been the beneficiaries.

Rabbon Gamliel emphasizes the three things one must explain at the *seder* table, listing *marror*, the symbol of bitterness and affliction after *pesach* and *matzoh*, the symbols of liberation. *Bnei Yissachar* applies the words of the *Alshich* to explain why *Rabbon* Gamliel employs this approach. Chronologically, we should mention the exile prior to the redemption. He explains that the bitterness which the Jews endured had a therapeutic effect and, therefore, we should not view it in a negative light. The pain and suffering, the bitterness and humiliation, rendered them worthy to receive the Torah. Indeed, only after they were liberated, after they experienced the *pesach* and *matzoh*, did they realize the true effect of the *marror*. The *geulas Mitzrayim*, exodus from Egypt, is a *direct* result of the *galus,* exile. We could not have experienced one had the other not occurred.

This idea should constantly be on our mind as we confront life's many challenges. We must be patient and trust that whatever Hashem does, whatever His decree for us, He has a purpose. The greater goal can only be effected by the phase which we are presently enduring. Hashem gives us the strength to withstand His trials. We have only to call upon our "reserves" and maintain the fortitude in order to emerge triumphant.

Target Your Gratitude

ואילו לא הוציא הקב"ה את אבותינו ממצרים הרי אנו ובנינו
ובני בנינו משעבדים היינו לפרעה במצרים

Had not the Holy One Blessed is He taken our fathers out from Egypt, then we, our children and grandchildren would still be enslaved to Pharaoh in Egypt.

*T*he *Baalei Mussar* explain that even had Pharaoh one day released us from bondage, we would still remain indebted to him. After all, did he not "liberate" us from servitude? Now that Hashem had redeemed us, we have no debt of gratitude to anyone but Hashem. *Horav Chaim Friedlandler, z"l,* supplements this idea. Had Pharaoh acquiesced to Moshe's demand that *Bnei Yisrael* be released from Egypt we might be grateful in some manner to Pharaoh. Hashem wanted *Bnei Yisrael* not to become subservient to anyone but Him. Consequently, He created a situation where it was obvious that only Hashem, without any "assistance," took us out of Egypt.

The problem of misplaced gratitude is real. All too often we thank everyone else and attribute our success to other sources, neglecting the true source of all good – Hashem. Nothing happens unless Hashem wills it. No man can achieve success unless it is Hashem's decree. All too often we are subjected to events and circumstances that do not seem related. We do not realize that every event that occurs has a distinct connection to the other. One day however, we will see how it all fits together. In the *Talmud Kiddushin 70 a, Chazal* say that in *Olam Ha'bah* there will be a history book which was written by *Eliyahu Ha'Navi* and signed by Hashem. Mankind will be given the opportunity to study and understand the purpose of all events and circumstances of men's lives. Our life experiences will all be inscribed there. Every ambiguity will be clarified. All the events which we had thought were purposeless – or even tragic– will take on a new meaning as they are interpreted in light of the continuum of history. We will then become acutely aware that it is Hashem Who really deserves our complete and undivided gratitude.

A *Midrash* teaches us the significance of directing our gratitude to its true source. Moshe *Rabbeinu* was forced to run away from Egypt as a result of the action he took against an Egyptian who was striking a Jew. When it became known that Moshe had killed the Egyptian, he was forced to flee the country for fear of his life. He came to the land of *Midyan*. One day as Yisro's daughters were being harassed by a band of ruffians, Moshe quickly stepped in and dispersed the would-be attackers. When the girls came home, they told their father, Yisro, that an "Egyptian man" had rescued them. The common explanation is that

Moshe was dressed as an Egyptian. Consequently, they thought that it was an Egyptian who had intervened on their behalf.

The *Midrash* interprets the expression in a somewhat different manner by first citing a parable. A man is bitten by a wasp and runs to the river to cool off the stinging bite. Arriving at the river, he sees a child drowning and jumps in and saves him. The child tells the man, "If not for you, I would have drowned." The man replies "If not for the wasp, I would not have been here to save you." When Yisro's daughters thanked Moshe for saving them he told them, "Do not thank me; thank the Egyptian that I killed. If not for him, I would not be here today."

The message is clear: We thank everyone, but the one who set the course of events to occur in such a manner that we would benefit. So who should we thank, the individual who was there or the One Who caused him to be there? If *Bnei Yisrael* had departed from Egypt with misdirected gratitude, it would have undermined the entire Exodus, and distorted its historical and spiritual lesson.

The Omnipotent Source

וכל המרבה לספר ביציאת מצרים הרי זה משובח

The more one tells about the Exodus, the more praiseworthy it is.

*H*orav Mordechai Gifter, shlita, adds a new insight to the concept of *Sippur Yetzias Mitzrayim*, telling the story of the Exodus. He cites the *pasuk* in *Shemos, 10:2, "And so that you may relate in the ears of your son and your son's son that I made a mockery of Egypt and My signs which I placed among them – that you may know that I am Hashem."* This *pasuk* teaches us an important aspect of the Exodus. Amidst the wonders and miracles, is the fact that Hashem forcibly limited Pharaoh's ability to act as a sensible human being. It is critical that we recognize that Hashem made a fool of Pharaoh and a mockery of Egypt. This fact in itself is a miracle!

Hashem demonstrated that He controls the course of nature; the lifestyle to which we are accustomed is apt to change if He so desires.

Moreover, Hashem has taught us that the *tzurah*, form, of a human being, his ability to think rationally, his capacity for making a logical choice between right and wrong, originates from Hashem. If man has become so evil that Hashem takes away this humanness, man becomes nothing more than an animal. He becomes a mockery! Pharaoh's refusal to permit the Jews to leave, his obstinacy to respond to Hashem's command, caused Hashem to revoke his faculty to be an intelligent human being. The lesson is simple. Man should never make the mistake of thinking that he is an end unto himself, that he has the power to do whatever he desires. Hashem, the source of all power, can take everything away from him in the blink of an eye!

All Through the Night

מעשה ברבי אליעזר ורבי יהושע ורבי אלעזר בן עזריה ורבי עקיבא
ורבי טרפון שהיו מסבין בבני ברק והיו מספרים ביציאת מצרים
כל אותו הלילה

It happened that Rabbi Eliezer, Rabbi Yehoshua, Rabbi Elazar ben Azaryah, Rabbi Akiva, and Rabbi Tarfon were reclining (at the Seder table) in Bnei Brak. They spent the entire night discussing the Exodus...

*W*hat is the significance of this story? Is there a special lesson to be derived from the fact that they discussed the Exodus all *night*? Was it really necessary to specify the *Tannaim* that were involved in the discussion? The *Ozrover Rebbe z"l*, addresses these questions, responding with a simple, but profound, explanation. Two levels of redemption took place in Egypt. There was the liberation from slavery, the physical redemption. The second represented a more sublime release, spiritual emancipation. The Jew was no longer subject to the prevalent moral degeneration that reigned in Egypt. He was free to serve the Almighty, free to lead a life replete with spiritual opportunity. He could build a life that valued the eternal, a life of values, morals, and decency, a life of *Torah* and *mitzvos*. To be freed from physical bondage only to be exposed and subjected to the Egyptian lifestyle, to be challenged by the *yetzer hora*, evil inclination, at every step and turn, does not represent true freedom – at least not for the Jew. Consequently, spiritual freedom was not only important, it was imperative.

This is the reason that emphasis is placed upon discussing *Yetzias Mitzrayim* at night. *Bnei Yisrael* were permitted to rest at night. There was no forced labor. The debauchery of the Egyptian culture, however, permeated the air twenty-four hours a day. The spiritual bondage continued throughout the night. The fact that the *Tannaim* discussed the Exodus all through the night, underlines this concept. The spiritual freedom was of greater significance. What better time to focus upon the spiritual bondage than at night, when physical servitude does not constrain spiritual expression? Yet, the Jews were restricted in this expression because the *tumah,* spiritual contamination of Egypt was all-pervasive.

The *Tannaim* who participated in this *Seder* had special reason to focus their discussion upon the spiritual aspect of *Yetzias Mitzrayim*. Had they themselves been in Egypt they would not have been enslaved. Rabbi Eliezer *ben* Azaryah was a *Kohen*, Rabbi Yehoshua was a *Levi*, Rabbi Akiva's father was a *ger tzedek*, and Rabbi Tarfon was a *Kohen*. Thus, the author of the *Haggadah* specified their names. These *Tannaim* were discussing the actual *Yetzias Mitzrayim*, the liberation that freed us from spiritual extinction.

No Shortcuts in Toiling for Torah

אמר רבי אלעזר בן עזריה. הרי אני כבן שבעים שנה ולא זכיתי
שתאמר יציאת מצרים בלילות עד שדרשה בן זומא.

*Rabbi Elazar ben Azaryah said, " I am like a seventy-year-old man
and I have not succeeded in understanding why the Exodus from Egypt
should be mentioned at night, until Ben Zoma explained it.*

orav *Yĕchezkel* Levenstein, *z"l* makes an insightful observation. Rabbi Elazar *ben* Azaryah merited significant recognition. He became *Rosh Ha'yeshivah* literally overnight, ascending to the position of leadership over his peers. Even his physical appearance miraculously changed. One merit, however, was not granted to him – the ability to find convincing proof that the Exodus should be mentioned at night. Why? If he was worthy of so many gifts, why did this *drashah* elude him?

We derive from here an important lesson: the only way one merits to become proficient in *Torah* knowledge is through toil and study. There are no shortcuts in the path to success in *Torah* erudition. One becomes a *gadol ba'Torah*, through *ameilus ba'Torah*, toil in *Torah* study, determination and diligence, not by sitting back waiting for it to happen. Rabbi Elazar *ben* Azaryah was worthy of miracles, but proficiency in *Torah* comes only to those who have worked specifically to achieve this goal.

Four Sons: Recognizing Children's Individuality

כנגד ארבעה בנים דברה תורה ... אחד חכם, ואחד רשע, ואחד תם,
ואחד שאינו יודע לשאול

The Torah speaks concerning four sons; a wise one, a wicked one, a simple one, and one who is unable to ask.

So much has been written and said concerning the *arba banim*, four sons. Ostensibly, we can derive an important message from their inclusion in the *Haggadah*. We suggest that they present a simple, but profound lesson. People are blessed with children; some are gifted and bright; some act evil and obnoxious; some are just simple nice children who "go with the flow" and are really not very concerned with anything that is intellectually challenging; and then there are children who take no initiative whatsoever.

The *Baal Haggadah* seems to be teaching us two significant principles that apply to parents as well as teachers. First, you cannot ignore a child, regardless of his attitude or religious perspective. We derive this from the fact that the *ben rasha*, wicked son, is included among the four sons. How many of us are guilty of this tragic offense? What happens if a child of ours does not live up to our standards or ח"ו becomes alienated from *Yiddishkeit*? Do we simply forget about him as if he does not exist? Do we not count him among our children or withhold our love for him? The *Haggadah* teaches us that *every child* deserves and should receive a response, regardless of his or her nature. Ignoring a child is tantamount to murder! This is especially critical, since, the parent has probably inadvertently contributed to his child's delinquency. Secondly we note the varied response to each individual child. We are taught in *Mishlei 22:6, Chanoch la'naar al pi darco*, "Educate a child according to his way." All children are not the same and must be dealt with individually, in accordance with their own unique nature, and personalities. The overall objective in education is the same, to raise a child to be a G-d-fearing responsible member of the Jewish community. Practically speaking, however, the specific goals may be different for each individual child. We must try to set realistic goals for our children and aim for these goals, by working with the child toward its realization.

Horav S.R. Hirsch, z"l, suggests a somewhat different meaning to this *pasuk*. "Raise the boy according to the course he will take when he is grown." We must be realistic in raising our children according to their future lifestyle and vocation. We must prepare them for what they will become. Our conception of the potential course their life will take should determine the form of education they will receive. For wealthy parents to raise their children in an affluent lifestyle is fine as long as the child will be fortunate enough to have the financial wherewithal to maintain this lifestyle. Similarly, sheltering a child from the outside world, sequestering him from the culture outside the *Torah* camp is wonderful and *necessary* if he will never have reason to venture out. If one day life requires the child to confront a world completely different from the one in which he was raised, how will he respond? Consequently, *we* must personally guide him to know how to live in a world that is antithetical to *Torah* – and survive spiritually. We must prepare our children for the future. We can determine which of the four sons will symbolize the adult our child will become by the way we rear them. The ultimate responsibility is ours.

The Wicked Son – Cynicism Denied/Torah Prevails

רשע מה הוא אומר. מה העבודה הזאת לכם ... ואף אתה הקהה את שניו ואמר לו בעבור זה עשה ה' לי בצאתי ממצרים

The wicked son, what does he say? "What does this service mean to you?"... So tell him bluntly: "This is done on account of what Hashem did for me when I came out of Egypt."

*T*he *ben rasha's* statement originates in the *Torah*, *Shemos 12:26*, where it is stated, *"And it shall be when your children say to you, 'What is this service to you? You shall say it is a Pesach offering to Hashem, Who passed over the houses of the Bnei Yisrael ... and the people bowed their heads.'"* In comparing the statement in the *Haggadah* with that in the *Torah*, we note that the response of each is different. The *Torah* states that the reason for the service is related to *Bnei Yisrael's* reprieve from death in Egypt. The *Haggadah* seems to be more blunt in expressing the reason for performing the service. Second, *Chazal* teach us that the Jews bowed down in gratitude and joy after hearing the news that they will bear children. The question is obvious. Is having a wicked son a blessing? Is a wicked son a source of gratitude or, rather, embarrassment?

Horav Eliyahu Meir Bloch, z"l, suggests that the answer that we find in the *Haggadah*, *"This is done on account of what Hashem did for me when I came out of Egypt,"* is included in the *Torah's* statement, *"You shall say it is a Pesach offering to Hashem Who passed over the houses of the Bnei Yisrael."* In making this statement, the *Torah* is not, responding to the wicked son. Rather, the *Torah* is acknowledging the secret of our people's continued existence. In passing over the Jewish homes, Hashem distinguished between Jew and non-Jew. He focused upon the individual, the minority who did not follow the wave of immorality that deluged Egypt. Hashem concentrates on the individual, sparing him despite his wicked environment.

As Hashem passed over the Jewish homes when He struck the Egyptians, so too will He seek out the righteous sons who will continue to perpetuate *Am Yisrael.* The *Haggadah* is blunt in response to the wicked son. The *Torah*, on the other hand, is responding to the people, enjoining them not to worry about the wicked sons. They will not bring us down. The *ben Torah* will persevere, laying the foundation for the continuity of our people. This was the good news that evoked the people's joy and gratitude. There will always be wicked sons who dispute and scoff at the *Torah* and its *mitzvos*, the rabbis and their customs. The cynics, however, will not defeat us. Hashem will pass over them as He continues to support and sustain us.

The Mind You Save May Be Your Own

מתחילה עובדי עבודה זרה היו אבותינו

At first our forefathers were idol worshipers.

oes mentioning our uncomplimentary origins serve as an inspiration to the reader? One would think that referring back to our roots might become demoralizing. *Horav Yechezkel Levenstein, z"l,* suggests that referring to our ancestors as idol worshipers gives us an understanding of why they repented. True, they were *ovdei avodah zarah,* idol worshipers, but at least they were involved in some form of *avodah,* service. They used their minds to think, involving themselves with spiritual ideas. Although they were mistaken in their belief they decided to establish some form of religion. Their primary sin was foolishly following what *they* thought was the correct path of religious observance. Consequently, it was not difficult to catalyze their return. Once they had one opportunity to be exposed to the truth, to be taught about Hashem and His *Torah,* they realized their error. The mind is very precious. As long as it is challenged and not controlled by one's passions, hope reigns that one will repent.

Regrettably, we do not always use our minds to think. More often, we "think" with our emotions. We follow our heart's desire, regardless of how irrational our actions may be. We are so absorbed in materialism, we no longer retain room for the appreciation of the spiritual. One should seek to fully utilize his mind, especially when his spiritual future is dependent on it.

The Bitter That Was Sweet

והיא שעמדה לאבותינו ולנו. שלא אחד בלבד עמד עלינו לכלותנו

It is this that has stood by our forefathers and us.
For not only one (enemy) has risen against us to annihilate us.

he *Sfas Emes* cites the *Zohar Ha'Kadosh* that says עבודה קשה, the hard labor to which *Klal Yisrael* was subjected in Egypt actually benefited them. They were involved in their work, to the extreme degree that they had no time or energy to socialize with their Egyptian neighbors. Had they not been subjected to slavery, they probably would have completely assimilated. With this in mind, the *Sfas Emes* interprets the "*Vhi*," it is this, to be referring to the actual slavery. The difficult labor which absorbed all of their time and drained all of their strength paradoxically helped them. It sustained them, protecting them from intermingling with the pagan Egyptians.

We never know what really is a gift from Heaven. At times, what appears to us to be a "difficult pill to swallow" is essentially a precautionary mechanism for our ultimate preservation. In explaining the "*Vhi She'amdah,*" the *Tiferes Uziel* uses an analogy which has a timeless application, especially in light of the suffering our people have experienced. A king once became angry with his only son, swearing that he would throw a large stone at him. Obviously once the king's anger was pacified, he regretted the oath that he had taken to throw this large stone at his only son. He questioned his advisors for a way out of his terrible predicament. They suggested that he grind the stone into little pebbles and throw them at his son. While he would still be fulfilling his oath, the stone would not cause any great harm, since it would have been broken up.

Hashem breaks up the stone of our *galus*, exile. If we were to receive the punishment which we are due, we could never possibly survive. Hashem, therefore, metes out the affliction of the exile in "spurts," so that we will be able to cope with it. This idea fits in beautifully with the second phrase of the "*V'hi She'Amdah.*" We say, "*For not only* one *has risen against us to annihilate us.*" Had there been only one stone/exile, we could never have survived. It is through Hashem's beneficence that the suffering has been broken up into bearable segments.

Anti-Semitism: Baseless Hatred

צא ולמד מה בקש לבן הארמי לעשות ליעקב אבינו

Go out and learn what Lavan the Aramean tried to do to our father Yaakov.

here is a purpose in learning about the anti-Semitism which existed in Lavan's home. The *Orzover Rebbe, z"l,* claims that the *Haggadah* is teaching us the reason the gentile has manifest hatred towards the Jew. Why did Lavan feel so negatively towards Yaakov? What harm, physical or financial, had Yaakov inflicted upon Lavan? Yet, Lavan sought to destroy Yaakov. Why? The answer is that there is no basis for Lavan's hatred. This is the lesson that the *Haggadah* is implying. There is no logical reason for anti-Semitism. Lavan did not benefit from hurting Yaakov. Similarly, the hatred to which we have been subjected for thousands of years is equally baseless.

Chazal tell us that it is a *halachah,* an absolute truth, that *"Eisav sonei l'Yaakov",* Eisav hates Yaakov. This *halachah* is immutable and not subject to discussion. It is a reality with which we must live. As the *Haggadah* states, in every generation another Eisav arises, another Lavan seeks to make our lives miserable for no apparent reason, other than the fact that we are Jews. However, Hashem is always present to protect us from destruction.

Lavan = Yetzer Hora

ולבן בקש לעקור את הכל. שנאמר ארמי אובד אבי

Lavan tried to uproot everything (of Yisrael), as it says:
"An Aramean sought to destroy my father."

he *Sifrei Chassidus* refer to Lavan *ha'Arami* as the *yetzer hora,* the evil inclination. The *yetzer hora* seeks every method to entice us to sin, very much like its alter ego, Lavan. What is the focus of this attempt? They explain that the *yetzer hora* has one objective, to sever the Jews' relationship with Hashem by destroying the recognition that Hashem is our Father in Heaven. When the Jew loses perspective of who he is – '*banim la'Makom,* children to Hashem – he no longer behaves appropriately. Hashem's essence, the way He relates to us, and, consequently, our relationship to Him, will save us from transgression. When we lose sight of these fundamentals, we are vulnerable to temptations.

Self-esteem and Dealing Wisely

Let us deal wisely with them.　　　　　　　　　　הבה נתחכמה לו

*T*he ability to enslave an entire nation of people requires a unique form of "wisdom." These were no ordinary people. *Bnei Yisrael* were greatly respected by the Egyptians. As descendants of the original tribes who came to Egypt, they enjoyed respect, admiration, and prominence. Their ancestor, Yosef, was Pharaoh's viceroy. How did their stature suddenly plummet to such a low degree that they were conscripted as menial slaves, performing harsh labor for the lowly Egyptians? Are we to believe that it was Pharaoh's "wisdom" that accomplished this feat?

The *Sforno* presents a new perspective in understanding the meaning of "dealing wisely" with the Jews. He claims that originally the Egyptians did not intend to enslave the Jews. Rather, they planned to make conditions so unbearable for them they would leave of their own volition. Sensitive to the public opinion of the other nations, the Egyptians attempted to rid themselves of the Jewish problem deviously. By indirectly confronting the Jews – through taskmasters who would afflict them — the Egyptians hoped that the Jews would choose to leave.

Horav Benzion Bruk, z"l, expounds on *Sforno's* words. The Egyptians were taken aback at the Jews response to the taskmasters. Instead of feeling anger and disgrace at being placed under taskmasters, the Jews agreed to build the treasure cities as a way of paying the tax. They did not fight; they did not argue; they did not offer any dissent. Where was their self-esteem? How did they permit themselves to be so cruelly degraded?

Pharaoh lacked the courage to drive out the Jews. Consequently, he created conditions by which the proud Jews would leave en masse. The Egyptians were convinced that the dignified Jews would never work at building treasure cities. Instead they taxed them financially. All they wanted from the Jews was tax money, which they hoped the Jews would refuse to give them. They relied on Jewish pride not to yield to such an indignity so that the end result would be the Jews emigration from Egypt.

This did not happen. Instead of leaving Egypt in dignified anger, they degraded themselves by consenting to build the Egyptian treasure cities. When the Egyptians saw how *Bnei Yisrael* had debased themselves, they added insult to humiliation and actually enslaved the Jews . The Jews' loss of self-esteem precipitated their downfall. Their decision to build the Egyptian cities was the catalyst that led to their total conscription as Egyptian slaves.

Self-esteem is more than a necessary character trait; it is an essential prerequisite for maintaining oneself on the high level of a *ben Yisrael*. We are confronted daily with challenges to our faith and tests of our belief in the Almighty. Only by maintaining our Jewish self-esteem, by proudly demonstrating our pride in being *bnei Torah*, will we succeed in not denigrating ourselves before the world. The weak submit; first on little issues. Later they are compelled to yield concerning issues that go to the core of their soul, issues that reflect our belief in Hashem and our adherence to His *Torah*. We have been bequeathed an unparalleled gift, the *Torah*. It should be our source of pride, the raison d'etre of our lives. The *Torah* is our greatest weapon against spiritual deterioration.

Who Is Consistently Consistent?

הבה נתחכמה לו פן ירבה ... ונוסף גם הוא על שנאינו

Let us deal wisely with them lest they multiply ... and they too may join our enemies.

*C*hazal tell us that Pharaoh had a council composed of three advisors, Bilaam, Iyov, and Yisro. Bilaam was the one who suggested the diabolical scheme to enslave the Jews. Iyov remained silent; he was later punished for his silence with ordeals of terrible pain and anguish. Yisro fled Egypt, rather than acquiesce to the evil advice. He was rewarded with the promise that his descendants would one day sit in the *Sanhedrin. This* well-known *Midrash* assumes a new meaning when one considers the nature of each of the three advisors and the inconsistency of their advice vis-a-vis each one's personal character.

Bilaam was as arrogant and egotistical as he was evil. He had the power to curse entire nations. He could cast anyone under his evil spell. Why did he fear the Jews to the point that *he* initiated the scheme to destroy them?

Iyov, a pacifist, was the symbol of loving-kindness and human decency. He could not tolerate evil; he would never turn his back on oppression. Yet, what did he do when the tragic decree to enslave an entire nation was made? He remained silent! Is that consistent with his nature? Is this the response we would anticipate from a man of his noble stature? Is silence the type of *reaction* one would expect from a man whose life was dedicated to humane causes? How could he tolerate the screams of the Jewish infants as they were cast in the river?

Yisro, the great philosopher, epitomized justice and truth. Was he acting in accordance with his nature? A man who had served — and subsequently rejected — every pagan idol, who had fought for integrity and justice, would be expected to decry such an evil decree. He should have protested vehemently, endeavoring to rescind the decree. Yet, what did this paragon of virtue, this noble fighter for justice do when he heard the tragic decree enacted against the poor Jews? He ran away! Is this type of behavior consistent with Yisro's character?

In light of the above, *Horav Yosef Zundel Salant, z"l,* infers a significant lesson. Hashem told Avraham during the *Bris bein Ha'besarim* that one day his descendants would go into exile. When Hashem issues a decree, *nothing* stands in the way of its fulfillment. Hashem's plan functions beyond the realm of the "consistent" and the "typical." Bilaam, who would typically not regard *Bnei Yisrael* as a national threat, acted strangely and advised Pharaoh to kill the Jewish boys. Iyov, whose essence could not tolerate cruelty, remained silent. Yisro, the fighter for justice, fled the country. Nothing can stand in the way of Hashem's decree. Indeed, the Egyptian exile and ensuing liberation are incongruous with the natural course of events.

Purposeful Degradation

וישימו עליו שרי מסים למען ענתו בסבלתם

They set taskmasters over them in order to oppress them with their burdens.

By inflicting hard labor upon the Jews, the Egyptians' goal was simply to destroy their dignity, to hurt them emotionally as well as physically. *Horav Shimon Schwab, z"l,* comments that the purpose of placing taskmasters over the Jews was to degrade and humiliate them, to convey to them that they could not be trusted to perform their job adequately without supervision. They were telling the Jews that the Jews were crude and undignified; their integrity was lacking and their work ethic unsuitable. Is there anything worse than such a loathsome form of emotional abuse? Yet, the intention of the Egyptians was to debase and degrade the Jews, to destroy their will so that they would become worthless human beings devoid of hope and aspirations.

This, suggests *Horav* Schwab, is the underlying meaning of the *pasuk* in *Sefer Devarim 26:6,*

וירעו אותנו המצרים, *And the Egyptians did evil to us.* "*Vayareiu*" can be interpreted as, "*And they made us look bad.*" They portrayed us as evil people, lazy ne'er-do-wells living off the Egyptians, people who could not be trusted. They maintained that we had no sense of allegiance to the country that admitted us and cared for us. They asserted that we were interested in dominating the Egyptian populace. When such foolishness is frequently reiterated, people begin to believe what they have heard. We can understand then why the Egyptians reacted in such a manner.

Tzaakah – Truth in Supplication

ונצעק אל ד' אלקי אבותינו

We cried to Hashem, the G-d of our Fathers.

The *Zohar Hakadosh* points out that among the various expressions used to describe an impassionate plea to Hashem, the most intense and most meaningful is *tzaakah.* This form of crying out is a supplication which emanates from the innermost recesses of one's heart. It is the essence of truth and reaches up to the source of truth — Hashem. The *Orzover Rebbe, z"l,* makes an analogy to lend deeper meaning to this idea.

In the *Mishnah, Meseches Keilim 17:13, Chazal* assert that if one makes skins from the hides of creatures that live in the sea, they are *tahor*, ritually clean and not susceptible to become *tamei*, contaminated. The sea dog, however is one sea creature that is not included in this law. The *Rosh* explains that for every creation on land, a counterpart lives in the sea. If a sea creature is under attack, he will not escape to land. Rather, he will submerge himself deeper into the sea. The sea dog, on the other hand, runs to the land. Since it identifies with the land in times of danger, it is categorized as a land creature. Although the sea dog *lives* in the sea, in times of stress it reverts to the land. According to *Chazal*, this indicates that the sea dog is essentially a land animal. The determining factor of its integral personality is where it turns in times of trouble, when its "real self" is manifested.

The same analogy applies to *Bnei Yisrael*. Some Jews have regrettably strayed from the path of observance, turned their backs on the religion of their ancestors, and betrayed the Almighty Who gave them *everything*. Are these Jews really gone? Have they permanently deserted their G-d and their people, or have they just fallen under negative influence? The answer, claims the *Orzover*, is dependent on to whom they turn in an *eis tzarah*, a time of anxiety and pain. In time of affliction usually the facade of arrogance is removed, the guise of indifference and cynicism fades away, as the real *pintele Yid* emerges, pure and untainted.

When the cry emanates from the Jewish heart, it demonstrates the real Jew, the one who really never turned away from Hashem. Where the Jew turns in his moment of affliction — and to Whom he prays in his time of need — determines the truth. *B   n*lived in Egypt, the center of moral degeneracy. They succumbed to a culture that was the antithesis of their belief and heritage. They "acted" like Egyptians. They seemed to have rejected everything Jewish. However, when the decrees against them surfaced from the nation which they had adopted, from a people who they foolishly believed accepted them, they turned to Hashem. They relied upon the G-d of their forefathers, the one Who has always been there waiting patiently for them, as a father waits for his child.

Three Redemptions –
Antidote to Three Slaveries

וישמע ד' את קלנו. כמה שנאמר וישמע אלקים את נאקתם

And Hashem heard our cry as it says, (Shemos 2:24): "And God heard their groaning."

he *pasuk* cited by the *Haggadah* indicates Hashem's *willing-ness* to respond to the cries of the Jews. After all, this is the likely response. The *pasuk* in *Shemos 6:5,* however, seems to say that it was the actual "hearing" (שמע) that was unique. The *Torah* says וגם אני שמעתי את נאקת בני ישראל *"Moreover, I have heard the groans of Bnei Yisrael".* Upon reading the text, one would think that the use of the word *"Ani",* "I (heard)" indicates that it was only Hashem Who heard *Bnei Yisrael* cry. If they had been groaning, why was it *only* Hashem Who heard? The *Noam Elimelech* explains that the groaning essentially had three manifestations.

The first type of cry emanated from the common Jew who had been subjected to backbreaking labor and to the affliction of the Egyptians throwing their baby boys into the Nile River. While most of the people cried over the demeaning and cruel slavery to which they were sub-jected, there were those, such as the tribe of *Levi,* upon whom no decree of hard labor had been issued. They lamented their lack of freedom. Their state of enslavement to Pharaoh was sufficient reason for them to mourn. Among the *Leviim,* a select group of individuals bemoaned their fate for a different reason. These were the *tzaddikim,* righteous Jews, who could not tolerate the effect of the slavery on their spiritu-ality. The suffering of their *neshamos* was greater than the physical hurt they endured. Their minds were not free to think; their hearts could not properly perform the *mitzvos* of the heart; their mouths could not express prayer for spiritual redemption, since they were compelled to pray for an end to the physical domination of the Egyptians. In short, these three areas of complaint represent the three perspectives of the Egyptian exile.

The *Noam Elimelech* says these three manifestations help to ex-plain the three types of redemption mentioned by the *Haggadah:* We thank Hashem for bringing us out of *"slavery to freedom, from darkness to great light, and from servitude to redemption."* Each Jew reflected upon his own personal liberation. The Jew who suffered harsh labor, toiling with brick and mortar, was grateful for his release from slavery to freedom. The *Levi,* who was not subjected to labor, thanked Hashem for redeeming him from his servitude. The *tzaddik,* who until now had bemoaned the darkness to which his *neshamah* was relegated, thanked Hashem for the new light.

The *Ohaiv Yisrael* supplements the words of the *Noam Elimelech.* While he agrees that the outcry took on three forms, this pattern was only manifest in the beginning of the servitude. After awhile, the Jews realized that it was not proper to bewail *only* their physical affliction. They should aspire to greater heights, crying out against the spiritual darkness that had enveloped their lives. They should cry about the spiritual muck in which their *neshamos* were submerged. Consequently, while they overtly lamented their miserable conditions, they also harbored an inner hurt, an intimate sorrow for their spiritual devastation. This affliction was not public. Its cry was unheard by all—except Hashem. Only the Almighty, Who knows and is sensitive to our internal emotions, heard this covert cry.

Myopic Vision

כל הבן הילוד היאורה תשליכהו.

Every son that will be born you shall cast him into the River.

Chazal tell us that Pharaoh's astrologers foresaw that the Jewish savior's downfall would occur as a result of water. They were even able to pinpoint the exact day on which Moshe would be born. Pharaoh's own daughter who found Moshe, took him home and raised him in the royal palace. Following the advice of his astrologers, on the day that Moshe was born, Pharaoh issued an edict to drown all male infants upon birth. The astrologers claimed that the threat of a Jewish savior had been averted. They were, of course, wrong, since Moshe's death was not caused by drowning, but rather by his involvement in the waters of *Merivah.* We may question the astrologers' actions. Since the sign that they saw actually alluded to another situation, how could they assume that once Moshe was placed in the Nile River, the sign from Heaven had disappeared? Obviously it was still present. Were they so myopic that the sign which they presumably saw yesterday had disappeared today—if it was alluding to something else? How could they say that they did not see the sign when it was apparently still present?

Horav Elyakim Shlesinger, shlita, infers a profound lesson from the astrologers' "myopia." A person can receive a clear vision from Heaven. Yet, if his perspective is distorted, he will either not see accurately, or will misinterpret the message. A person sees what he *wants* to see. One who wears blue-tinted glasses will always see blue, regardless of the actual color. His vision is tainted by the tint! As far as the astrologers were concerned, the downfall of the Jewish savior would occur with his drowning in the Nile River. Nothing else mattered, and no other sign would change their distorted perception. Myopic vision is very often not related to vision of the eyes!

A Child's Insights

כל הבן הילוד היאורה תשליכהו.

Every son that will be born you shall cast him into the River.

Pharaoh thought that the way to prevent the emergence of a Jewish leader was to drown all baby boys. Indeed, his astrologers had told him that the downfall of the Jewish savior would be effected through water. As a result of this decree, Amram, who was the *gadol ha'dor,* the spiritual leader of that generation, separated from his wife, Yocheved. Ostensibly, all Jewish men followed suit. Rather than bring boys into the world to be drowned by Pharaoh, they left their wives. Miriam, yet a young child, however, challenged her father Amram's decree. She claimed that his decree to separate was far worse than Pharaoh's, since he was also preventing the birth of girls. Moreover, Pharaoh was a mortal king, whose decrees would not outlast him. Amram was a *tzaddik* whose good deeds would protect him and his progeny. The piercing words coming from this young child made a powerful impression upon Amram. Consequently, he remarried Yocheved, and Moshe *Rabbeinu* was born.

Let us take a moment to analyze what happened. One would assume that we are describing the influence of a determined, but young, child. After careful perusal, we may note, comments *Horav Baruch Mordechai Ezrachi, shlita,* that the real credit should be attributed to Amram. He truly distinguished himself. The *gadol ha'dor,* the leader of hundreds of thousands of people, made a decree, and an entire nation accepted his word and followed his example. A little girl, his daughter no less, offered an insightful critique of his edict. What did this great leader do? Did he laugh it off? Did he ignore the little girl? No! He accepted her constructive criticism, annulled the decree, and remarried his wife! This unconditional acceptance represented true greatness! He did not argue; he did not attempt to present "his side" of the story, his reasoning for issuing the decree. He simply accepted Miriam's reproof. We must question what went through Amram's mind. What originally motivated him to make the decree, and what was it about Miriam's analysis of the circumstances that inspired him to rescind his order?

Let us begin by analyzing Miriam's critique, "Your decree is worse than Pharaoh's." What is the decree to which she is referring? Amram made no decree; he merely *responded* to Pharaoh's decree to kill the Jewish boys. We must, therefore, say that Miriam addressed an issue that went to the foundation of *Klal Yisrael's* existence. It is, in fact, an issue we must confront even today. Amram was about to nullify— or at least put "on hold"— a *mitzvah* of the *Torah.* The *Torah* commands us to *"Be fruitful and multiply."* It is the first *mitzvah* of the *Torah.* To ignore this *mitzvah* is to ignore the *Torah*—the foundation of our existence! Never has *Klal Yisrael* been without the *Torah.* We have never abandoned the *Torah,* despite the cruel pogroms, the persecutions and catastrophes to which we have been subjected as individuals and as a nation. It is the basis of our life! Therefore, how could Amram say, "Separate from your wives"? This was Miriam's critique. Amram was, by example, issuing a statement. If the situation warrants it, if the lives of your children are put in danger, then do not have children. Miriam questioned, "Is this not, however, contrary to the *Torah* which remains with us even during the most trying circumstances?" If the *Torah* commands us to have children, how could Amram *decree*, by example, that the situation in Egypt overrides the *Torah*? *Klal Yisrael* has undergone so many trying ordeals in their history, but *never* as a nation have they collectively forsaken the *Torah*. Was Pharaoh's decree any worse than the pogroms, the Inquisition, and the Holocaust that we survived as a nation—because we have adhered to the *Torah*?

This poignant – but compelling – critique prompted Amram to rescind his order to the Jewish men to separate from their wives. We never know when the innocent words of a young child can leave a remarkable impression. Perhaps we do not listen well enough.

True to Yourself and Your People

ויוצאנו ד' ממצרים ביד חזקה ובזרוע נטויה

And Hashem brought us out of Egypt with a mighty hand and with an outstretched arm.

The *Torah*, in addressing the *geulah*, redemption from Egypt, employs *arba leshonos shel geulah*, four expressions of redemption. They are:

והוצאתי אתכם מתחת סבלת מצרים ... והצלתי אתכם מעבדתם ...
וגאלתי אתכם בזרוע נטוי-ה ... ולקחתי אתכם לי לעם

I shall take you out from under the burdens of Egypt; I shall rescue you from their service; I shall redeem you with an outstretched arm...I shall take you to Me for a People. (Shemos 6:6,7)

These four expressions allude to the distinct stages of the Jews' liberation from the Egyptian exile. *Horav Gedaliah Schor, z"l,* posits that these expressions relate as equally to the individual and to the entire nation. Every person experienced his own personal redemption from the Egyptian culture. Every individual must liberate himself from the shackles of his own enslavement to the *yetzer hora*, evil inclination. He cites the *Sfas Emes*, who says that these expressions coincide with the four elements which comprise man: fire, water, wind and dust. The characteristics of these elements fuse together to create the emotional and physical composition of man, the *gashmius*. Man's body, his corporeal essence, is but a container into which the *neshamah*, soul, is placed. *Horav Chaim Vital, z"l*, says that these four elements of man are also the source of every negative character trait within man. Every bad *middah* originates in some manner from these physical components of man. The *neshamah*, spiritual dimension, is ensconced within the body as if it were in exile. The function of transcending the physical with the spiritual, by sublimating the physical dimension of man to its higher calling, is the process by which man "liberates" himself from his physical bondage. This is one's personal *Yetzias Mitzrayim*. We strive to transform these purely physical elements to serve Hashem, so that they become vehicles for spiritual development.

In four places in the *Torah* we are enjoined to relate the story of *Yetzias Mitzrayim* to our children. *Chazal* have derived from this apparent redundancy that children may be categorized into four groups, or "four sons." They are: the *chacham*, wise son; the *rasha*, wicked son; the *tam*, simpleton; and the *she'eino yodea lish'ol*, the child who does not even know what to ask. *Horav Yehudah Leib Chasman, z"l*, feels that these "four sons," actually represent four distinct personalities. The traits typified by these four sons represent the inner struggle within each one of us. There are moments when we act with wisdom, reflecting common sense and forethought. There are times when we "lose it," foolishly carrying on like the wicked son. There are times when we act like the simple son, unsure of the direction in which we should go, unclear as to the manner in which we should act. The last son, the one who does not know to ask, is never far from us. We can all relate to moments when we just do not know what, how, or whom to ask.

We must address these life situations in the same manner that the *Torah* responds to the individual sons. In keeping with *Horav* Schor's thesis that the four expressions apply equally to the individual, we may suggest another area of focus, the individual's unique tendencies. We are adjured to address those areas of our personality that are deficient. Likewise, as we find with the wise son, we must cultivate and enhance the areas in which we excel. This concept is underscored in the words of the *Hagaddah*, "In every generation it is man's duty to regard himself as though he personally had come out of Egypt." We are obligated to experience a personal liberation in which we elevate the physical, addressing those areas of our character which need improvement.

Changes – Not Necessarily
A Positive Sign.

ויוצאנו ד׳ ממצרים ביד חזקה ובזרוע נטויה

*Hashem brought us out of Egypt with a mighty hand
and with an outstretched arm.*

Was it really necessary to leave Egypt? Would it have created such a negative situation if Pharaoh had just halted the
slave labor and improved the living conditions for the Jews? Why did
Moshe not insist that things return to "normal," that Pharaoh rein-
state the Jews as common citizens? *Otzer Chaim* offers a simple, but
profound, response which carries a timely message. He recounts a
comment made by the *Chasam Sofer, z"l,* during the emancipation in
Austria. The prejudicial laws were lifted, enabling Jews to hold positions of importance and granting them access to society in general.
Everyone was excited about their newly-found freedom. The ghetto
Jew was history. The *Chasam Sofer,* however, was disturbed by the
turn of events. His students could not understand why everyone was
overjoyed, while their *rebbe* was weeping and depressed.

The *Chasam Sofer* responded with a parable. There was once a
very powerful king who found his senior officer and close confidant
guilty of a grave crime. Under the usual rules this officer deserved to
be executed. The king, a dear friend of this officer, commuted his
sentence to a long prison term. He told him that undoubtedly his tenure in prison would be extremely difficult, but he could retain ultimate
hope. The king would one day liberate the officer from his incarcera-
tion. He would just have to be patient and wait for that day.

The officer was exiled to a horrible prison and placed into a filthy
pit with scorpions and snakes. He was resigned to his misery amidst
a hostile environment. The only thing that kept him alive was the
king's assurance that he would one day be released. One day the hap-
less prisoner heard sounds outside of his pit. Exhilarated, he looked
up in anticipation; perhaps this was the moment he had so long
awaited. His heart pounded excitedly as the door was opened to al-

low the king's messengers to enter. "We have come to alleviate your condition. We are going to clean up your pit and make a window for your dungeon to permit some light to enter."

As soon as the prisoner heard these words, he emitted a piercing cry and began to weep uncontrollably. The king's messengers asked him incredulously, "Why are you weeping? You should be overjoyed with the changes that will be made to your dismal condition." "You do not understand," responded the prisoner. "The entire time I was incarcerated I knew that one day I would be freed. This awareness kept me going. It encouraged me, as it gave me a glimmer of hope that one day I would again have a normal lifestyle. Your appearance in order to clean up my pit unfortunately indicates that I will be here yet for a long time. My hopes of leaving here in the near future have been shattered."

"I, too, am crying," said the *Chasam Sofer*, "for I fear that this 'wonderful' equality we have just been granted is regrettably a message that the end of our exile is not so near. We have just had 'citizenship' in *galus* conferred upon us, and I should not cry?" In the *Talmud Sanhedrin 98a, Chazal* comment, '*If you see a generation whose persecutions flow like a river, wait for Moshiach.*' Our suffering is part of a process which purifies us as it prepares us for the Final Redemption.

Measuring Gratitude

ובאתות זה המטה. כמה שנאמר ואת המטה הזה תקח בידך אשר תעשה בו את האותות

With signs refers to the miracles performed with the staff, as it says (Shemos 4:17): "Take this staff in your hand, that you may perform the miraculous signs with it".

oshe *Rabbeinu* initiated the last seven *makos*, plagues, while Hashem told Aharon to strike the river and the earth to initiate the first three plagues. *Chazal* attribute Aharon's designation in performing these *makos* to the fact that the river and the earth had protected Moshe. He had been placed in the river as an infant to be concealed from the Egyptians. Later, the earth covered the Egyptian that he had killed. Moshe benefited from two inanimate objects. Therefore, he must demonstrate his gratitude. This seems to be excessive. The *middah* of *hakoras ha'tov*, appreciation, is one of the mainstays of character development, but was it necessary to show this gratitude to an inanimate object that was essentially fulfilling its purpose in the world? After all, the water or earth are not sensitive to a lack of gratitude.

Horav Mordechai Kukis, shlita, explains that in the area of *hakoras ha'tov*, the beneficiary need not make *cheshbonos*, calculations, to appraise the actual amount of effort his benefactor has exerted in order to estimate how much gratitude he owes: How much did the benefactor sacrifice to grant his favor? Did he have to do it anyway? Was he going my way? If we find that it did not really cost him very much we may discover many more excuses and reasons that could justify *not* repaying the favor – not demonstrating gratitude where it is due. Quite possibly, once we start with the *cheshbonos*, we might negate the whole concept of *hakoras ha'tov*!

This is the lesson we learn from Moshe. If Hashem had *insisted* that Moshe demonstrate his sense of gratitude, even to an inanimate object, how much more so must we show our appreciation to human beings, and – ultimately – to Hashem *Yisborach*, the source of all good. Our concern should not be from whom we have received a favor, or the size and value of that favor; our first and only consideration should be that we have benefited and should show our gratitude.

Horav E.M. Shach, shlita, goes a bit further in expounding the demand for *hakoras ha'tov*. We must recognize that Hashem is the source of all the good that we receive. The medium through which we receive this benefit is nothing more than a vehicle for channeling Hashem's favor to us. What difference does it make to us who or what Hashem employs to serve as the agent for carrying out His objective? He demands that we imbue ourselves with the *middah* of appreciation, not distinguishing among the benefactors. This is a case in which too much "discrimination" might cause us to lose sight of the actual source of our blessing – Hashem.

The Good Within the Bad

באתות זה המטה. כמה שנאמר ואת המטה הזה תקח בידך
אשר תעשה בו את האותות

With signs refers to the miracles performed with the staff, as it says
(Shemos 4:17): "Take this staff in your hand, that you may perform the
miraculous signs with it".

*T*he *mateh Elokim*, staff of Hashem, which Moshe carried, was
the instrument that initiated the various plagues which
assailed Egypt. One might think that this staff was "dedicated" for
effecting punishment and exacting retribution. We see in the *Torah*
that when the Jews arrived in *Marah* and were confronted with the
challenge of having nothing to drink, this staff served a different function. The *Torah* tells us in *Shemos 17:5, "And your staff, with which
you struck the river, take in your hand." Rashi* cites the *Mechilta* which
takes note of the *Torah's* emphasis on the staff *"with which you struck
the river."* When *Bnei Yisrael* were clamoring for water, Hashem said
to Moshe, "Take the same staff that you used to bring plagues upon
Egypt, and strike the rock with it, and water shall come out." Let *Bnei
Yisrael* see that the same staff which brought about plagues can also
bring good. No dichotomy exists between the staff that brings evil
and the one that brings good. Hashem is the source of both, and from
Him only good emanates. We do not always perceive the good within
the "bad." We do not always perceive that out of sorrow and suffering emerges joy and happiness. It is necessary to have faith that the
staff of evil will effect good. Indeed, the good is there – we have only
to recognize it.

We may use yet another approach to understanding the words of
Chazal. Every situation/occurrence which we experience, be it sad
and tragic or festive and joyful, comes from Hashem for a specific reason. Consequently, we must recognize the good, as well as the bad.
Chazal teach us not to attribute the bad to another source. No, the
good and the bad are both present to serve a purpose – to sanctify
Hashem's Name and to inspire us to take note.

In referring to *Tisha B'Av*, our day of sorrow, Yermiah *Ha'Navi*
calls it *"moed,"* a word which is usually used in reference to a festival.

This seeming inconsistency is explained by *Horav Avraham Yitzchak Bloch z"l* in the following manner: The word *moed*, מועד is derived from the word *vaad*, ועד, which means appointment. A *moed* is thus a time set aside when Hashem has an "appointment" with the world, when His presence and greatness are manifest.

Hashem's eminence can be acknowledged from two distinct perspectives: Through the miracles of redemption with the joy and happiness they bring; and through destruction with its pain and sorrow. The glorious exodus from Egypt inspired a nation to perceive *gadlus Ha'Boreh,* the greatness of Hashem, the Creator. Likewise, the devastating *churban,* destruction of the *Bais Hamikdash* with the ensuing slaughter of Jewish life, was such a catastrophic tragedy that it could only have occurred as part of a Divine plan. These two distinct empirical moments in history, *geulah,* redemption, and *churban,* destruction, were both appointments with Hashem, moments when His presence was uniquely manifest. The staff of evil and the staff of good are one and the same. We only have to perceive its message. Our task is to uncover its positive/constructive message.

The Means Should Reflect the End

Blood, Frogs, Lice...   דם, צפרדע, כינים

It was Aharon who initiated the first three plagues. Hashem delegated this reponsibility to Aharon, because Moshe was not permitted to strike the water or the dust. The water protected him when he was an infant, while the dust concealed the Egyptian that Moshe killed. It would have shown ingratitude for Moshe to strike either the water or the ground. Imagine, Moshe and Aharon were involved in the most sublime endeavor of their lives – taking *Klal Yisrael* out of Egypt – but the overriding concern was to be careful not to "offend" an inanimate object, because it once had been a vehicle for protecting Moshe!

The captains of the "ship" who were securing its release from the muck of Egypt were concerned with steering clear of anything tainted with a vestige of impropriety. The greatness of man is measured by his ability to maintain the highest level of rectitude, even while he is involved in the noblest of endeavors. While Hashem was liberating *Klal Yisrael* from the moral degeneracy that was Egypt, it was imperative for Moshe to remain sensitive and aware of the gratitude he owed — even to an inanimate creation of Hashem.

Horav Mordechai Kukis, shlita, makes the observation that the *Torah* is averse to the popular dictum, "the end justifies the means." Rivers of blood and seas of tears have been spilled on the altar of this ideal. Whether it is in the name of kashrus, *Shabbos*, or Jewish education, our goal-oriented society somehow does not seem to take into account the methods with which it achieves its aim. It is of no concern who gets hurt, how many lives are ruined, or whose reputation becomes besmirched, as long as our objective is realized.

Horav Kukis reminds us of a common occurrence, the removal of the *Sefer Torah* from the *Aron*. Instantly, a sea of people move toward the *Torah* to demonstrate respect and kiss its mantle. Some individuals push their way through the crowd, at times knocking over elderly men, stepping on toes, just so they can express their love for the *Torah*. Of course, they apologize all along, as they continue inflicting their damage upon anyone whose misfortune it is to be in their path.

Moshe *Rabbeinu*, the *Rabbon Shel Kol Yisrael*, demonstrated sensitivity to an inanimate object, even while he was involved in *Klal Yisrael's* deliverance from Egyptian bondage. How much more so should we be vigilant in our interaction with others — even in the midst of performing a *mitzvah*.

The Challenge of Kiddush Hashem

Blood, Frogs, Lice...   דם, צפרדע, כינים

ach of the *makos* had its own unique effect on Pharaoh. The plague of frogs, however, had a different component. This plague had a "human interest" element which teaches us an important lesson in the area of Jewish responsibility. *Chazal* teach us that it did not take long for Pharaoh to beg Moshe to implore Hashem to put a halt to the swarms of frogs that were literally infesting his entire country. Moshe prayed to Hashem, and the frogs all died. *Chazal* tell us that the frogs who had entered the ovens miraculously did not die, either in the oven or afterwards! We may question the remarkable reward received by the frogs. After all, Hashem commanded them to enter the ovens, where else should they have gone? A similar question may be asked regarding *Chazal's* statement in the *Talmud Pesachim* 53b. *Chazal* tell us that Chananyah, Mishael and Azaryah entered the fire as a result of a *Kal V'chomer*, a fortiori argument, which they derived from the plague of frogs. They said, "If the frogs were willing to sacrifice their lives to sanctify Hashem's Name, so should we." The question is obvious. The frogs had no other choice but to conform to the will of Hashem. Why are they lauded for doing precisely what they were supposed to do?

Horav Shimon Schwab, z"l, remarks that Yechezkel *Ha'navi* had actually advised Chananyah, Mishael and Azaryah to run and hide. Their response was straightforward; they sought to prove a point. If they had fled, people would say that everyone, including the Jews, had bowed down to the idol. By accepting the challenge and risking their lives, they were demonstrating to the world that the Jews had rejected the idol. This was the appropriate time to make a statement against Nevuchadnezzar. They certainly could have run away in order to save themselves. However, their cowering before the wicked king would be, in effect, a statement in his support, that he was in control.

What motivated them to accomplish this supreme act of self-sacrifice? What inspired them to go forward rather than backward? The frogs who went into the ovens were well aware of the obvious results. *Horav Schwab* explains the rationale. The frogs were *all* commanded to swarm throughout Egypt. They knew that this also included entering the burning ovens. They *all* had the choice to go where they desired. This unique group of frogs understood that if some of them would choose not to enter the ovens, then Hashem's decree would appear ineffective. This action personified their *mesiras nefesh*, self-sacrifice. They did not have to go into the ovens; they *wanted* to go into the ovens, they felt it was important.

Chananyah, Mishael and Azaryah drew a parallel to their own situation. They could escape and be spared, but what about the humiliation it would eventually have caused to Hashem's Name? What about the degree of success, the renewed power over the people of which Nevuchadnezzar would be the beneficiary? They could not permit this. Therefore, they acted accordingly and entered the fire.

How often do we have the opportunity to sanctify Hashem's Name, but do not because it is inconvenient? How often does the opportunity present itself to perform a *mitzvah,* but we ignore it because it does not "appeal" to us? True, we can pick the easy *mitzvos,* the ones that give us public acclaim, the ones that will not demand too much sacrifice on our part. We should not be surprised, however, when Hashem rewards us accordingly.

Submission at Last!

Locusts   ארבה

While the *Torah* emphasizes the importance of transmitting the entire story of the exile and exodus from Egypt, it attaches special significance to *makas Arbeh,* the plague of locust. Indeed the *Torah* commands us to relate to our children and grandchildren how Hashem made a mockery of Egypt specifically during this plague. Why?

What is the significance of the plague of locusts that it has become the focus of transmission to future generations? *Horav Simcha Zissel Broide, shlita,* observes that the dialogue which ensued between Moshe and Pharaoh was not limited to *Bnei Yisrael's* release from Egypt. Moshe was also using this forum to demonstrate to Pharaoh the identity of Hashem, the Master of the world. It was Pharaoh who audaciously challenged Moshe with the words, "Who is Hashem that I must listen to His voice?" Pharaoh denied the existence of a Supreme Being Who directed the world. The miracles and wonders that occurred in Egypt were "lessons," with which Moshe sought to imbue Pharaoh with an awareness that Hashem is the Creator and Ruler of the earth and all of Nature.

The first plagues did not seem to have a great effect upon Pharaoh. He remained resolute in his denial of Hashem, renewing the zeal with which he enslaved the Jews. As the plagues progressed, the pain and affliction which he and his people suffered became increasingly difficult to endure. Thus, Pharaoh summoned Moshe and Aharon to put a stop to the plagues. His pleas were always accompanied by the same false, vacuous promises of freedom for the Jews. As soon as each plague ended, Pharaoh reneged on his word, persecuting the Jews with heightened vigor.

Pharaoh appeared to his nation to be an all-powerful king whom no one could vanquish. Even if he "seemed" to give in to the effects of the plague, it was only a transitory change. Indeed, immediately after the plague had ceased, Pharaoh returned to his previous stance.

This ruse continued for the seven plagues which preceded the plague of locusts. Now, in the aftermath of the plague of locusts nothing was left! All of the crops and greenery had been totally obliterated. No longer did Pharaoh have to beg Moshe to rescind the plague; the locusts retreated of their own accord because nothing was available for them to eat. Pharaoh no longer had reason to display a show of strength, for he had nothing to gain. The plague had run its course, and he and his people were devastated. Now Pharaoh retreated, meekly crying out, "I have sinned to Hashem." Pharaoh had seen the effects of total destruction. He could only hope that his repentance would avert a new calamity. He was like a child who has been hit by a stick many times. The fear of an upraised stick was sufficient to frighten him into submission.

The idol had fallen! Pharaoh's subterfuge had halted abruptly. The mighty ruler who feared no one was now scared of his own shadow. The plague of locusts had finally put Pharaoh in his place; he had finally reached his breaking point. It forced him to shed his arrogance, exposing the fraud that he had perpetrated against his people.

Are You Your Own Worst Enemy?

וירא ישראל את היד הגדולה אשר עשה ד' במצרים וייראו העם את ד'
ויאמינו בד' ובמשה עבדו

And Yisrael saw the great hand which Hashem laid upon the Egyptians, and the people revered Hashem, and they believed in Hashem and in His servant Moshe.

t seems that the people did not become secure in their belief until the Egyptians had drowned. They retained the fear that they might have to "go back." This idea is expressed by *Sforno* in his commentary regarding the four expressions of redemption employed by the *Torah* to describe the various stages of *Yetzias Mitzrayim*. The four *leshonos shel geulah* as interpreted by *Sforno* are: "והוצאתי" "I will bring you out," when the plagues begin, the slavery will end; "והצלתי" "I will save you," when you leave their borders; "וגאלתי" — I will redeem you," with the drowning of the Egyptians in the Red Sea. After the death of your oppressors, you will no longer be slaves; "ולקחתי", " I will take you unto Me as a nation," at *Har Sinai* with the giving of the *Torah*.

We must attempt to understand *Sforno's* words. Although *Klal Yisrael* were incarcerated in Egypt for hundreds of years, they remained descendants of a noble and dignified lineage. Why did they need to *see* their master's demise before they could *feel* a sense of freedom? Should not the many miracles performed *by Hashem – for them* – have been sufficient cause to establish their personal trust in Him? Would not the idea of leaving the shambles of Egypt (after the *Makos*) be adequate reason to end their insecurity? Why was another step necessary to dislodge their original slave mentality from their minds?

Horav A. Henach Leibowitz, shlita, derives a significant lesson about human nature from *Sforno's* words. We are our own greatest enemy. Once an individual has made up his mind about himself, it is very difficult to undo. The bad impression we have of ourselves can be one of the greatest deterrents to our self-development. Once one has a low image of himself, either self-imposed or created by others — be it teachers, parents, or friends – it is extremely difficult to transform that picture. Although *Bnei Yisrael* were liberated from Egypt, they still remained slaves, in their minds. They were not free *men*; they viewed themselves as freed *slaves*. They were afraid of the image that was etched in their minds of their cruel oppressors. It was necessary for them to see the Egyptian corpses washed up onto shore to impress upon them the point that they were finally free men.

Horav Leibowitz posits that this feeling extends to one's spiritual persona. In fact, probably the most common cause of spiritual deterioration is the lack of appreciation for one's own greatness. When the *yetzer hora,* evil inclination, coerces us to sin it says, "You can do it. You're just an ordinary guy. You do nothing special. Your sin will not make much of a difference, anyway. Leave the *Torah* study and *mitzvah* observance to those who are spiritual giants not to the plain guy, like you." Every Jew must recognize his own self-worth and the love that Hashem has for him as an individual. If we would only realize that we are princes, created in the image of Hashem, the idea of sin would be unfathomable. Our self-image and our sense of pride should deter us from sin.

As we sit at the *Seder* table, we recall the Exodus and the events leading up to that special moment, the giving of the *Torah.* These milestone occasions should elevate our self-image and bring about the realization that we are the children of Hashem. How can a son possibly rebel against such a loving Father? How truly fortunate are we to be endowed with so much. It is simple questions such as these that will guide us to appreciate how special we are, imbuing us with a greater understanding of our responsibility to observe *mitzvos.*

Internalize and Eternalize

ועל הים מה הוא אומר.
וירא ישראל את היד הגדולה אשר עשה ד' במצרים

However, (of those miracles) at the Sea, the Torah relates that
"Yisrael saw the great hand which Hashem laid upon the Egyptians..."
(Shemos 14:31)

The *Midrash* explains that *Klal Yisrael* were privy to remarkable spiritual revelations as they stood on the shores of the Red Sea. Indeed, *Chazal* tell us that a common maidservant was able to perceive greater revelations of the *Shechinah* than Yechezkel Ha'navi! This is derived from the word "*zeh,*" "this," from the phrase "*Zeh Keli V'Anveihu,*" "*This is my G-d and I will glorify Him*" *(Shemos 15:2).* The Jews were able to point with their fingers to the awesome sights they were experiencing. Yet, as *Horav Shalom Schwadron, shlita,* notes, the maidservant remained a simple maidservant in spite of her exposure to such exalted spiritual vision. In contrast, despite the fact that Yechezkel did not experience all there was to see, he remained a *navi.*

What happened? Why did so many, who saw so much, relinquish the effects of their unparalleled experience?

Horav Schwadron recounted this *Chazal* in the presence of *Horav Meier Chadash, z"l.* He added his own inferences, stating that as life proceeds complacency often takes hold of an individual, causing him to forget even an extraordinary experience. *Horav Chadash* took issue with this statement. In order to reinforce his contention with what seemed to be the logical explanation of *Chazal*, he cited an incident that occurred to him personally. When he was a young man in Russia, just before the first World War, Russian soldiers caught him without his required papers. This was a period in which the gentiles did whatever they chose, treating the Jew as some type of lowly parasite. The desire for Jewish blood was unleashed. Quickly, the soldiers determined that this young Jewish man was guilty of treason and deserved to be executed. They prepared the firing-squad to execute their decision. Sensing the hopelessness of the situation, *Horav Chadash* nervously began reciting *Vidui* and *Krias Shma*.

The soldier in charge of the squad demanded that *Horav* Chadash stand erect and not fidget, since he was making it very difficult for the soldiers to aim accurately. Overcome with fear, the *Rav* trembled, shaking back and forth. Once again, the soldier called out to him harshly to stand straight. This time, the soldier's scream awakened the Russian general who was taking his afternoon nap. He took one look outside and immediately scolded the soldiers for the terrible thing they were about to do. The soldiers quickly dispersed, and the *Rav* was saved.

"One would think," continued *Horav* Chadash, "that after such an incredible experience, life would not be the same. After a little while, however, I began to notice the captivating power of complacency, and I realized that I was falling prey to this 'affliction'. I was losing sight of the amazing miracle that had saved me from certain death. Immediately, I made up my mind to grasp hold of the 'past' and transform it into the 'future,' forcing myself to remember the miracle. I made every effort to solidify and strengthen my belief in Hashem, recognizing that if He desires that I remain alive, then *nothing* whatsoever will be an obstacle. I reviewed this notion constantly, never forgetting the past, seeking every opportunity to translate what had happened in the past into the present and future."

Believing Is Seeing

וייראו העם את ד׳ ויאמינו בד׳ ובמשה עבדו

And the people revered Hashem, and they believed in Hashem and in Moshe His servant.

A Jew should strive to attain such a sublime level of *emunah* in Hashem, that he truly believes with a clarity of vision. Let us explain. People accept the notion that "seeing is believing." This means that in order to really believe, one must actually see the phenomenon. Hence, belief in a given concept is a step lower than actually seeing it. This is not the *Torah* perspective. The *Chidushei Ha'Rim* asserts that as *Bnei Yisrael* stood at the shores of the Red Sea and experienced unprecedented miracles, they were privy to a revelation of Hashem which was unparalleled. The *Torah* states that first *Bnei Yisrael* "saw" miracles and only afterwards did they "believe" in Hashem. Their visual perception was insufficient. Their *emunah* which followed was the epitome of conviction. *Emunah* is faith so strong that one actually senses its reality.

We see this phenomenon in practice. The most erudite secularist will concede that our "eyes" make mistakes. That which we perceive as reality is often a figment of our imagination. One example is the color of the ocean. Take a picture of the ocean and it will appear to be blue. Standing at a distance, gazing at the ocean you will see blue. We know however that water has no color. The blue we see is the reflection of the sun against the water. Hence, seeing is not believing! Believing, true *emunah*, however, should be an unshakable and unmistakable form of vision.

Sfas Emes expounds upon this idea, questioning the "need" for the word ויאמינו, they believed, after ויירא, they saw. What advantage is there in believing after one has seen a spectacle and visually confirmed his belief? He responds that *emunah* is the *application* of what one sees and believes into the heart and mind of the individual, so that it becomes a resolute part of the person's ideological conviction. When one has *emunah sheleimah,* perfect faith, he is imbued with a perception that does not falter with the blandishments of the *yetzer hora*, evil inclination, or the vicissitudes of trial and travail. His belief constitutes this perception of reality! Seeing is not believing. Believing, however, takes what one sees and makes it "real."

Remembering the Past to Appreciate the Future

God has bestowed many favors upon us   כמה מעלות טובות למקום עלינו

*G*ratitude and appreciation are virtues that are not simply praise-worthy, they are essential traits. On the *Seder* night, we are enjoined to recount the many wonders and miracles that Hashem wrought for us. *Ibn Ezra* contends that appreciation goes a step further. We are to remember how it used to be, how we suffered, the pain and affliction to which we were subjected, the thirst and hunger which accompanied us, and the depression and hopelessness that ruled our lives. Hashem rescued us from all that. He took us out of misery, granting us the opportunity to live as free people.

Horav Mordechai Gifter, shlita, explains that one must appreciate and give gratitude where it is due. Does one, however, analyze the good that he has received? Does one ever think about what life would have been like had he not been saved? Do we ever really evaluate the good? Do we simply say "thank you" and continue with "business as usual"? One must remember what it had been like; think back to the days of misery and pain, feel some of the frustration and grief that *used* to be so much a part of his life. Then and only then will he truly understand the essence of the favor he has received. All too quickly, we pay our respects to our benefactor and forget about him. If we pay more attention to our past, we might more fully appreciate the present.

This, according to *Horav* Gifter, is the purpose of the *"Da'yeinu"* format of the *Haggadah*. We must delve deeper into the "good" that we have received, reviewing it, analyzing every aspect of it, so that we will experience greater appreciation at the present time.

The First Step

And (He) split the Sea for us.   וקרע לנו את הים

*B*nei Yisrael were trapped between the approaching Egyptian army and the menacing waters of the Red Sea. What did their leader, Moshe *Rabbeinu,* do? He prayed; he implored Hashem to spare the young nation whom He had just liberated from Egypt after two hundred and ten years of persecution. Hashem responded to Moshe's supplication in a manner which we must attempt to understand. The *Torah* records Hashem's words to Moshe, *"Why for do you cry out to Me? Speak unto the Bnei Yisrael that they go forward."* (*Shemos 14:15*)

Rashi explains Hashem's response to Moshe as he stood in supplication before Him. Hashem told Moshe, "Now, when *Bnei Yisrael* are in distress is not the appropriate time to prolong prayer. Let them go forward. The merit of their forefathers and their own *emunah*, faith, which they have exhibited are sufficient reason for the Sea to split before them." This interpretation is enigmatic. Moshe was praying to Hashem during a time of severe crisis for *Bnei Yisrael*. Hashem told Moshe that now, when *Bnei Yisrael* were teetering on the brink of disaster, was not a time for prayer. Is there a more propitious time to entreat Hashem, than when there is danger? How else should Moshe have confronted the problem, if not by praying to Hashem?

Horav David Shneur, shlita, infers a profound lesson from this "dialogue." People often declare that if Hashem would only remove all of the obstacles which prevent them from seeing Him properly, they would commit themselves totally to His service. This is not the sequence of events necessary to serve Hashem with devotion. Man must make the first move, take the first step toward spiritual commitment; Hashem will complete the process. This was Hashem's imperative to Moshe, "Why are you standing here praying for *Bnei Yisrael*? Let them go forward and do something! *Bnei Yisrael* have sufficient merit to justify the splitting of the Red Sea for them." It was essential for *Bnei Yisrael* to take that proverbial "first step;" the rest would become history. Prayer must serve as a positive form of communication with Hashem, not as an excuse for deferring our acceptance of responsibility. We must pray, and we must do. Hashem will respond to our actions.

Krias Yam Suf: A National Miracle

וקרע לנו את הים והעבירנו בתוכו בחרבה

And (He) split the Sea for us; He led us through it on dry land.

The splitting of the Red Sea was a remarkable miracle. Is there a parallel event in Jewish history? Was it truly the only time that water "deferred" to man? Indeed, in the *Talmud Chullin 7a,*

Chazal recount an incident in which R' Pinchas *ben* Yair was on the way to perform the *mitzvah* of *pidyon shevuyim*, redeeming Jewish captives. He came to a river that was impassable. He commanded the water to split, so that he could pass through. The river responded, "You are performing the command of your Master, and so am I. You *might* be successful in your efforts to rescue the hostage, while I am assured of success. What makes you think that your *mitzvah* takes precedence over mine?" R' Pinchas *ben* Yair, responded, "If you do not split immediately, I will decree upon you that all of your water should dry up!" The river split, and R' Pinchas *ben* Yair passed through. *Chazal* summarize the story with the observation that R' Pinchas ben Yair's power was equal to that of Moshe and all of *Klal Yisrael*.

Keeping this in mind, the *Sfas Emes* wonders how *Krias Yam Suf* demonstrates the singular greatness of *Klal Yisrael*. After all, did a similar miracle not occur for an individual? He offers a profound response. Certainly, Hashem can alter the course of nature for a single *tzaddik*. The righteous have extraordinary merits which grant them access to miracles. When, however, did Hashem alter nature for an entire nation? The *chidush*, novelty, of *Krias Yam Suf* was that an extraordinary miracle took place for an entire nation. This phenomenon demonstrated to the world the *kedushah*, holiness, of *Am Yisrael*—not just the individual Jew—but the totality of the nation!

Horav Tzadok Ha'kohen,M'Lublin, z"l, supplements this thought. The miracle of *Krias Yam Suf* exhibited *Am Yisrael's* innate *kedushah* to the world. After all, what virtue did the Jews display that made them more worthy to be spared than the Egyptians? They had sunk to the nadir of depravity, to the forty-ninth level of *tumah*, spiritual impurity. What distinguishes one idol-worshiper from another? The answer is that while externally the Jews may not have displayed a spiritual demeanor that would merit *Krias Yam Suf*, their inner being, their *penimius*, was inherently holy.

Don't Worry – Trust in Hashem

וקרע לנו את הים ... וספק צרכנו במדבר ארבעים שנה. והאכילנו את המן

And (He) split the Sea for us .... And He provided for our needs in the desert for forty years; and fed us the manna.

*O*ne miraculous occurrence followed another. Is there a relationship between the two? *Chazal* seem to think so. They say in the *Talmud Pesachim 118a*: *"A man's sustenance is as difficult as the splitting of the Red Sea."* Simply providing man with sustenance is as great a feat as *Krias Yam Suf*. The *Zohar Ha'kadosh* questions *Chazal's* statement. Is there any act that is difficult for Hashem to perform? Was *Krias Yam Suf* difficult for Hashem? Is it difficult for Hashem to sustain a person?

A number of explanations address this *Chazal*. The *Chozeh M'Lublin, z"l,* suggests a profound insight. *Chazal* are not focusing their observation upon Hashem. They are, rather, speaking to man concerning which path to take when life becomes more demanding. Earning a living is — by any standard — a complex endeavor. It demands great fortitude and commitment. It requires determination, resolution, and — most importantly — faith in the Almighty. What does one do when the situation is bleak, when prospects for success are — at best— limited, when every way one turns the door to success seems to be closed?

Chazal's message is to follow the lesson of *Krias Yam Suf*. The Jews were trapped. They could expect either dying at the hand of the Egyptians or drowning in the Red Sea. What should they do? They had no other choice but to be *boteach b'Hashem*, trust in the Almighty. They turned to Him in the hope that He would spare them. With this hope and trust, they entered the threatening waters of the Red Sea to be saved by Hashem. Likewise, when we are faced with the challenge of *parnassah*, livelihood, trusting humans is ineffectual. Absorbing one's mind and even one's soul in the anxieties that accompany the quest for *parnassah* is wasteful and detrimental to both one's physical *and* spiritual health. Only one approach will achieve success —*bitachon, true* trust in Hashem. If one truly believes that Hashem will help him, He will.

Horav Simcha Bunim, M'Peshischa, z"l, gives a similar response with a slightly different twist. At the *Yam Suf*, the Jews had no idea how they would be rescued. In fact, the splitting of the Red Sea was probably the last thing they expected to happen. With regard to *parnassah*, Hashem sends salvation from a source that, for the most part, is unanticipated. We have no idea from where Hashem will bring about our sustenance. Our obligation is to trust that He will.

Morality vs. Hypocrisy

And (He) drowned our oppressors in it.　　　　　ושקע צרינו בתוכו

*T*he *Torah* emphasizes that the Egyptian soldiers died *together* with their horses and chariots. *Rashi* cites the *Midrash* which asks the obvious question: Where did the Egyptians get horses with which to chase the Jews? Were they not all killed during *makas barad*, when hailstones rained down and destroyed everything in their path? The response is that these horses belonged to the select Egyptians who were "ירא את דבר ד'" — *"feared the word of Hashem,"* and had removed their animals during the hailstorm which was the seventh plague. The horses which belonged to these G-d fearing Egyptians had been endangering Jewish lives. This *Midrash* clearly satirizes the "G-d fearing" Egyptians. They feared Hashem when the lives of their horses were at stake, but they openly defied Him when the issue was Jewish survival. This blatant hypocrisy has challenged our people throughout history. The same people who professed religion, love, and fear of G-d acted towards the Jews with utmost hatred, treating them cruelly, brutally inflicting upon them the greatest atrocities, all in the name of religion! We must endeavor to explain the sanctimonious fear of G-d which the religious Egyptians displayed.

In the sphere of morality, Hashem is the source of ethics for three reasons. First, and most basic is "יראת העונש", fear of punishment. Man must obediently submit to Hashem's service as a result of his fear of retribution for transgression, as well as his anticipation of reward for being moral and upright. *Chazal*, however, have always spoken disparagingly of those who do not move beyond this stage by aspiring to a higher level of service to Hashem.

We consider the next two characteristics prerequisites for developing proper motivation towards serving Hashem. They are "יראת הרוממות", fear of awe – or man's awareness of Hashem's overwhelming greatness – and ultimately "אהבת ד'", love of Hashem. Although "awe of Hashem" compels obedience and submission to Him, the *Torah* demands that we aspire to attain "love of Hashem." These concepts, which arise out of the recognition that Hashem is the source of absolute value, establish the basis and foundation of moral law. The

G-d fearing Egyptians were only able to reach the first stage; fear of retribution. Hence, the *Torah* states that they were "ירא את דבר ד'". They feared Hashem's word, they were fearful only of His "word", His actions, but they were not in fear of "Him". This "fear" was nothing more than cowardice, which was quickly transformed when they felt that they were no longer in danger. One must possess all the qualities of fear and love of Hashem in order to maintain the appropriate moral balance.

Livelihood – Finding Favor

ספק צרכנו במדבר ארבעים שנה והאכילנו את המן

He provided for our needs in the desert for forty years, and fed us the manna.

nei Yisrael had been liberated from the slave labor of Egypt and rescued from certain death either at the hands of the Egyptian Army or the waters of the Red Sea. They were now confronted with a new challenge, the challenge of *parnassah*, earning a livelihood.

Chazal have traditionally referred to *Parashas Ha'mann* as the *parsha* of *parnassah*, livelihood. The underlying concept of *bitachon*, trust in Hashem, is the motif of *Parashas Ha'mann*. In essence, we should reflect upon every aspect of our daily bread and recognize its true source. If one is acutely aware of Hashem's providence, he *never* pursues any type of questionable or inappropriate endeavor in his quest for livelihood. An individual who resorts to cheating, trickery, dishonesty, and fraud, may try to maintain all outside appearances of a devout Jew. Alas, he is not truly devout. His belief in Hashem's unlimited power to provide for each of His creations is not sufficiently strong. He demonstrates a sanctimonious form of *kefirah*, blasphemy.

In a lecture, *Horav Shimon Schwab, z"l*, cites a wonderful concept from *Horav S.R. Hirsch, z"l*. In the *tefillah*, prayer, *Ashrei* which we recite three times daily, one *pasuk* alludes to livelihood פותח את ידך ומשביע לכל חי רצון, *"You open Your hand and satisfy the desire of every living being."* Indeed, if we fail to say this *pasuk* with proper *kavanah*, concentration, we must repeat it. This is required so that we fully accept in our minds the idea that Hashem provides adequately for all living creatures.

Horav Hirsch questioned the meaning of the phrase משביע לכל חי
רצון. It should read משביע רצון לכל חי, "He satiates the desire of all
living creatures" or משביע ברצון כל חי, "He willingly satiates all living creatures." The word רצון seems to be "misplaced." *Horav Hirsch*
explained that the *ratzon* here is related to the expression *"Yehi
Ratzon,"* that our request be רצוי לך, pleasing to You. We should understand the word *ratzon* in our prayers in this perspective. This
concept consequently becomes the essence of our *tefillah* for livelihood.
We entreat Hashem to enable us to find *ratzon*, grace and favor, in
the eyes of others.

Horav Schwab implies that *parnassah* represents the direct inter-
vention by which Hashem bestows *ratzon* upon an individual. This
response cannot be coerced or gained through manipulation. Our
success (or lack thereof) in earning a livelihood is contingent totally
upon Hashem, the source of all *parnassah*.

A Perfect Partnership –
Hashem and You

וספק צרכנו במדבר ארבעים שנה והאכילנו את המן

He provided for our needs in the desert for forty years, and fed us the manna.

*B*nei Yisrael were privy to an unprecedented array of miracles,
ranging from the Ten Plagues to the many miracles that occurred during the Exodus, to the splitting of the Red Sea. The Jews
clearly saw that Hashem was with them during times of crisis. However, was this the most crucial lesson? Or is there another miracle
which, although less profound in nature, has a more significant message? *Horav S.R. Hirsch, z"l,* observes that *Bnei Yisrael* were acutely
aware that Hashem was close to them during the critical stages of their
development. What about their recognition of Hashem's role in their
everyday necessities? This was the lesson of the miracle of the *manna.*
Hashem takes into account the needs of *every* human being. One can—
and should— rely upon Hashem for his sustenance.

All of the amazing supernatural phenomena that accompanied *Bnei
Yisrael's* exodus from Egypt, even *Krias Yam Suf,* all faded in signifi-

cance when *Bnei Yisrael* confronted the stark reality of impending hunger menacing their families. *Horav Hirsch* declares that this concept is reflected in *Chazal's* dictum, *"It is as difficult to provide man's sustenance as it is to split the Red Sea."* The threat of hunger looms over man, undermining every principle and abrogating every resolution. Indeed, as long as the overwhelming anxiety of *parnassah*, earning a living to support one's family, envelops a person, he cannot achieve his potential in *Torah* study.

How does one free himself from the tentacles of this tension? One must acknowledge that the concern for providing for man's material needs does not ultimately rest on man. In fact, it does not depend upon him at all! Man must acknowledge the fact that he can do only his own part, but ultimately he must depend upon Hashem for success in his endeavors. It is his duty to *endeavor* to provide sustenance for his family, but he must be convinced that every single human being is ultimately sustained by the Almighty.

The one who does not "accept" Hashem as the sole Provider is bound to toil away his days, laboring to ensure himself and his dependents material support. He will do anything to achieve his goal. He will compete ruthlessly; he will cheat if necessary; he will fall prey to any scheme regardless of its shady nature, just in order to earn sufficient money. The pursuit of money can become an obsession, a demanding, unrelenting and ruthless contrivance that has the power to destroy many lives.

Hashem sought to cure the young nation of this malady. He led the people into a stark, barren desert where they felt the anxiety, where the material requirements of the present were inaccessible, and where the prospects for the future were dubious. They saw for themselves what the obsession to earn a living can do to an individual. Until now, they did not worry about the next day; they had been slaves for masters who provided them their daily sustenance.

Now Hashem was establishing the rules for obtaining one's sustenance. He would provide *Bnei Yisrael* with their daily bread. They were taught that whatever they needed would be provided, neither more nor less. They did not have to worry about the morrow, for Hashem would provide for tomorrow. They merely had to trust Him.

Only after they had exhibited unreserved confidence in Hashem could they be assured that His *Torah* and *mitzvos* would be observed, with no unrealistic anxiety about material hardship interfering with their *avodas* Hashem. The individual whose overriding concern in life is, "What shall I have to eat tomorrow?" has no place in the panorama of Jewish belief. One's persistent concern for his *material* future will ultimately lead him astray from Hashem and His *Torah*. It would serve us well to be more concerned about our spiritual future and leave the material dimension to Hashem.

Hashem's Eternal Love

רבן גמליאל היה אומר כל שלא אמר שלשה דברים אלו בפסח
לא יצא ידי חובתו ואלו הן — פסח, מצה, ומרור

Rabban Gamliel used to say: Whoever has not explained (said) these three things on Pesach has not fulfilled his duty, namely, Pesach, Matzoh, and Marror.

Certainly, *Rabban* Gamliel's intention was not for us to simply "say" these three words. His point is that we should explain the implications and lessons to be derived from these three symbols to the best of our ability. The first symbol we introduce for discussion is the *Korban Pesach*. Why did we eat the *Korban Pesach*? What special miracle did it commemorate? It recalls the "passing over" by Hashem of the Jewish homes during *makas bechoros*, the killing of the firstborn. If we think about it, would it ever enter anyone's mind that Hashem would kill the Jewish firstborn? After all, the purpose of the plagues was to effect the release of the Jews from Egypt, not to kill them.

Ostensibly, the goal of the *makos* was to rescue the Jews from exile. Which Jews are we actually discussing? After two hundred and ten years of exposure to Egyptian culture, with its immorality and degenerate behavior, were the Jews really that distinct from the Egyptians? Was the *Yiddishe neshamah*, the *pintele Yid*, that apparent, or was it hidden under years and years and layers and layers of repulsive spiritual degeneration? Indeed, the *Baalei Kabbalah* write that had the Jews remained a bit longer, they would never have been worthy of redemption. This is the stinging criticism that the *Sar shel*

Mitzrayim, Egypt's guardian angel, rained upon the Jews as they stood by the shore of the Red Sea. "These are idol worshipers (referring to the Egyptians) and those (referring to the Jews) are also idol worshipers." What distinguished the Jew from the Egyptian, so that the Jew should live while the Egyptian should perish?

It is specifically for this reason that we emphasize the miracle of "passing over" the Jewish homes. We were not spared as a result of overt righteousness and virtue. It was not our positive deeds and devotion to the Almighty that earned us liberation. It was Hashem's eternal love for us that gained us salvation. Externally, according to our actions and behavior, we may appear to have a strong similarity with the Egyptians, their culture and lifestyle. Inwardly, however, there *is* something, a spark, a non- extinguishable ember, that makes it impossible for this bond of love to be severed. The most significant miracle is that Hashem demonstrated His love for us. This is the foundation for all of the miracles of *Yetzias Mitzrayim*. Is it any wonder that *Rabban* Gamliel insists that we publicize and explain it?

Bitachon's Barometer

פסח ... על שום שפסח הקב"ה על בתי אבותינו במצרים.

Pesach ... it is because the Holy One Blessed is He, passed over the houses of our fathers in Egypt.

The uniqueness of the manner in which *Bnei Yisrael* ate that first *Korban Pesach* in Egypt is expressed by the *Torah*, in *Shemos*, 12:11: "So shall you eat it: Your loins girded, your shoes on your feet, and your staff in your hand; you shall eat it in haste."

The manner in which they ate the *Korban Pesach* reflected *Bnei Yisrael*'s readiness for immediate journey. In his commentary, *Sforno* emphasizes their *bitachon*, trust in Hashem. He writes, "They demonstrated their implicit trust in Hashem by preparing themselves for the road while they were still in prison." *Horav Moshe Schwab, z"l,* takes note of this remarkable trust in the Almighty. *Bnei Yisrael* had been subject to such inhumane servitude for hundreds of years that they no longer knew the meaning of the word "freedom." Even after

Moshe had notified them of their imminent redemption, they still continued to function under the same conditions of harsh slavery as they had before.

The miracles that appeared and disappeared did not seem to leave a permanent impression upon Pharaoh. Obviously, *Bnei Yisrael's* trust in Hashem was not a result of their own perception, it was the product of pure *bitachon* in the Almighty. Moshe relayed Hashem's message to *Bnei Yisrael*. They responded immediately, preparing for the *geulah*, liberation, while they were still incarcerated in Egypt.

This implicit trust, this unequivocal reliance upon Hashem, is the touchstone of *bitachon*. This attitude imbues us in this final *galus*, as we *await* the advent of *Moshiach*. Everything we do, wherever we go, should reflect the same "*chipazon*," haste, as we exhibited when we prepared for the auspicious moment of our redemption from Egyptian slavery.

All too often, we forget our real purpose on this earth. *Horav Schwab* cites an anecdote from the *Chafetz Chaim* which clearly communicates our mission in this world. A Jew once came to visit the *Chafetz Chaim* and was surprised by the overwhelming poverty in the house. He asked the *Chafetz Chaim*, "Pardon me if I am presumptuous, but where is your furniture?" The *Chafetz Chaim* responded by questioning the visitor, "And where is your furniture?" "I," responded the guest, "am only a visitor here." The *Chafetz Chaim* retorted, "So, too, am I only a visitor in this world. Therefore, I do not concern myself with setting up more than temporary accommodations." We must all remember that we are in this world only with "visitor" status, as we await that clarion call of the *shofar* which will herald our final redemption.

Life – The Greatest Gift

ואמרתם זבח פסח הוא לד׳ אשר פסח על בתי בני ישראל במצרים

You shall say, "It is a Pesach-offering for Hashem, Who passed over the houses of the Bnei Yisrael in Egypt."

The festival commemorating our exodus from Egypt, our liberation from the most cruel bondage, is called *Chag Ha'Pesach*, the Festival of Passover. This name recalls how Hashem "passed over" the Jewish homes during *makas bechoros*, when the Egyptian firstborn were killed. Considering the nature of the festival and the focus of its commemoration, the name seems to be a misnomer. Would it not have been more appropriate to call the festival, *Chag Ha'cheirus*, the Festival of Freedom? This was no ordinary redemption. It was a liberation from a cruel and intense slavery. The Jews were ensnared by the guile of the Egyptians. First, Pharaoh promised a reward for each brick that they made. The Jews set about, resourcefully, to make as many bricks as they could, only to find out that this had become their daily quota! Then Pharaoh stopped giving them straw with which to make the bricks. Every move that Pharaoh made was intended to destroy Jewish pride and dignity, to transform a holy people into dispirited and crass beggars, who had no purpose and no future. Why then, do we not call the festival dedicated to commemorating the Jews' release from the abyss of Egypt the Festival of Freedom?

Nesivos Ha'mussar derives a profound lesson from the alternate choice of name—*Chag Ha'Pesach*. There is no greater *chesed*, kindness, than sparing an individual from death! Once the destroyer had been granted permission to strike, no distinction existed between Egyptian and Jew. When the *middas ha'din*, attribute of judgment, reigns, no human can stand before it and live. This is consistent with the words of David *Ha'melech* in *Sefer Tehillim 130*, "*If you preserve iniquities, oh G-d, Hashem, who could survive?*"

The kindness of sparing an individual from death is so great that it overshadows *all* of the miracles, wonders and salvation that occurred in Egypt. Even the actual liberation pales in comparison. Being given access to life, being spared from a premature demise, incorporates within it *all* of the preceding benefactions. What value is freedom when one has no future?

Those who do not appreciate the true meaning of life may grasp its peripheral aspects, but remain totally oblivious to its essence. We view life as a medium—as a vehicle for attaining joy and pleasure. We talk about various goals for which life is worth living, while we fail to recognize that the greatest joy is inherent in life itself. This idea is best reflected in the words of David *Ha'melech* in *Tehillim 118*, "*Hashem has caused me to suffer terribly, but He has not given me over*" *to death."* In this psalm, David *Ha'melech* looks back on a life filled with pain and suffering. Yet, he is able to thank Hashem for the greatest gift—the gift of life.

Horav Chaim Shmulevitz, z"l, points out two aspects of life that constitute its essence. First, only by living and performing *mitzvos* does one have the opportunity to receive reward in *Olam Ha'bah*. The greatest pleasure that one can attain is closeness to Hashem. Only through our humble existence in this world can this potential be realized. A second aspect of life which is invaluable is the opportunity to interface with one's fellowman, to share in his joy, to help shoulder his sorrow. The opportunity to give of oneself to others is man's greatest gift. Indeed, it infuses life with its greatest meaning.

Constancy and Consistency in Serving Hashem

מצה זו שאנו אוכלים על שום מה? על שום שלא הספיק
בצקם של אבותינו להחמיץ

Why do we eat this matzoh? It is because the dough of our fathers did not have time to ferment.

*C*hametz and *matzoh* symbolize two opposites with two sets of different laws. The *mitzvah* of *achilas matzoh* is only required the first night of *Pesach*. The prohibition against eating *chametz* continues for all seven/eight days of *Pesach*. In order to fulfill the *mitzvah* of *matzoh*, the dough must be guarded *l'shem mitzvas matzoh* with a special intent for the *mitzvah*. The fermentation of grain into *chametz*, on the other hand, is prevented simply by keeping an eye on the clock, making absolutely sure that the time of leavening has not passed. We find a significant punishment imposed upon one who eats *chametz* on *Pesach*. The amount necessary to incur this punishment is not the usual *kazayis*, olive, but rather a *ma'shehu*, a tiny insignificant amount. Why is there such a disparity between the two, and what is the lesson to be derived?

Pesach represents *emunah*. This learning experience taught us to believe in Hashem Who directs and governs the world and the lives of its inhabitants. We were privy to an unprecedented revelation of Hashem's might and power. Bearing this idea in mind, *Horav Moshe Schwab, z"l,* distinguishes between *chametz* and *matzoh* and the concepts each represents. When one defers to the blandishments of his *yetzer hora,* evil inclination, and sins, he is called a *baal aveirah,* a sinner. If he intentionally sins, he is a *rasha,* a wicked man. Despite his impropriety, he is still not viewed as the ultimate evil doer — an *apikores,* apostate. He has not yet lost his portion in *Olam Ha'Bah.* Conversely, if one observes *all* the *mitzvos* of the *Torah* meticulously, yet, he is prepared to state that any dictum of *Chazal* is an exaggeration and not applicable, he is deemed an *apikores.* In areas of *emunah* the slightest infraction is devastating. Any deviation, regardless of how negligible, carries with it the onus of apostasy.

Emunah means total sublimation of oneself to Hashem *Yisborach.* To devote *almost* all of oneself, but hold back even a *ma'shehu* is *apikorsus.* This may be analogous to one who proclaims he is about to jump into the ocean. He jumps, but he is still held up by a very thin wire attached to his body. Is this considered jumping into the water, or is it nothing more than fraud? This is the difference between all of the *aveiros* and the *aveiros* pertaining to matters of faith. Concerning all other sins, man falls prey to his desires; he is not able to overcome the *yetzer hora's* seductive powers. This makes one a sinner, but he has not revoked his belief in Hashem. In the area of *emunah,* one who does not believe severs his relationship with Hashem. He becomes an apostate.

How does one make *chametz?* He doesn't make *chametz;* it just happens . *Chametz* is the result of "pausing," halting momentarily in the process of making dough. Indeed, if one were to knead dough all day without stopping it would not become *chametz.* Only if one pauses the length of time that it requires to ferment does it becomes *chametz.* The underlying rationale behind the prohibition of *chametz* is that one must constantly strive to serve Hashem. There can be no lapse in one's service and devotion to the Almighty. If there is a lapse in one's *avodas* Hashem it becomes *"chametzdik."* He interjects himself into the picture. He pushes Hashem away.

A child's nature is to be constantly occupied. Activity is the mask of a child. As he matures, the *yetzer hora* gets a foothold on his personality. Suddenly alacrity and perseverance yield to indolence and haphazardness. By nature, man is a doer; he seeks to work. When he slows down, he contradicts his natural tendency.

The *mitzvah* of *achilas matzoh* supplements the prohibition against eating *chametz*. While *chametz* symbolizes a lapse in *avodas* Hashem, *matzoh* introduces us to the idea of being "on guard," seeking to use every minute to serve Hashem. The lesson of *matzoh*, the concept of being assiduous in *mitzvah* performance, is a positive lesson that can be communicated at a single time — on the first night of *Pesach*. For if one does not eat the *matzoh*, he transgresses. That in itself communicates the message of constant growth. By refraining from *chametz* a single time, however, one does not necessarily capture the lesson of *chametz*. One must reiterate the lesson for seven days and refrain from eating *chametz*, so that the *experience* of not eating will leave an indelible mark in his mind. He will truly understand then that one cannot tolerate a lapse in his belief in Hashem.

Haste for a Reason

מצה זו שאנו אוכלים על שום מה? על שום שלא הספיק
בצקם של אבותינו להחמיץ

*Why do we eat this matzoh? It is because the dough of our fathers
did not have time to ferment.*

Among all of the *mitzvos* connected to the festival of *Pesach*, none is so stringent as the prohibition of *chametz*. One who does not recount the story of the Exodus, one who does not eat *matzoh* or *marror* has "only" neglected performing a *mitzvah*. One who eats *chametz*, however, is liable to the Heavenly punishment of *kares*, premature death. This harsh punishment seems to underline the significance of the *mitzvah* of *matzoh*. The prohibition against eating or keeping *chametz* in one's possession indicates the critical importance of the haste in which the Jews left Egypt. They departed in such a hurry that the dough which they were making did not have the opportunity to rise. Imagine, in the space of eighteen minutes, the amount of time it takes for dough to become *chametz*, all of *Klal Yisrael* left Egypt!

Does this speed minimize the miracle of the exodus from Egypt? Would the significance of *Yetzias Mitzrayim* have been diminished if the Jews had left Egypt in an hour or even two? Did eighteen minutes really make such a difference?

Horav Avigdor Ha'Levi Nebentzahl, shlita suggests that the concept of *chametz* is spiritual in nature. *Bnei Yisrael* were totally absorbed in the degenerate Egyptian lifestyle. They were so mired in the contamination of Egypt that had they remained just a bit longer, they would never have been able to leave. *Bnei Yisrael* had descended to the forty ninth level of spiritual impurity. They were at the brink of ultimate disaster. They were about to become Egyptian citizens – forever!

This is the concept that the *Torah* first and foremost seeks to impress upon us. The underlying motif behind the prohibition against eating *chametz* is that the Jews were almost at the brink of spiritual annihilation. We were "raised up" from this nadir of degeneracy, to *cheirus pnimis*, internal liberation, and spiritual freedom. Never would *Bnei Yisrael* return to that lowly position of near spiritual extinction. As they viewed Egypt then, they would no longer see it again. True, they would err and sin, but they would never sink to the point of utter depravity that they did in Egypt.

Klal Yisrael's deficient level of spirituality became apparent during the *makas bechoros*, when the firstborns of the Egyptians were killed. The *Baal Haggadah* tells us that it was Hashem Who passed through Egypt on that fateful night. Only Hashem – not an angel – could discern between Egyptian and Jew. The area of differentiation between Egyptian and Jew had narrowed so much, as a result of the Jew's spiritual degeneration, that an angel would not have been able to distinguish between the two.

We find that at the *Yam Suf*, the angels complained to Hashem, "Why do you spare the Jews while the Egyptians are drowning? These are idol worshipers, and those are idol worshipers! What advantage do the Jews have over the Egyptians? They are both sinners."

This idea, claims *Horav Nebentzhal*, is the *Torah's* message for us. The *halachah* is stringent regarding *chametz*, prohibiting leaven which distinguishes itself from *matzoh* in a matter of minutes. Between leaven and non-leaven — between the *matzas mitzvah* and the prohibited *chametz* — is a mere minute! The *Torah* seeks to impact upon us a profound message. Between *nitzchiyus*, eternity and spiritual oblivion, between *kedushah*, holiness and *taharah*, purity, there is a distance of only one minute. One *ma'shehu*, minuscule drop, determines the essence of an individual. Had *Klal Yisrael* remained in Egypt *for one more minute* they would have been relegated to spiritual oblivion. A *geulah*, redemption could not have occurred. One more minute! That is the difference between *chametz* and *matzoh*. Eighteen minutes constitutes the creation of *matzas mitzvah*. One more minute and the individual becomes liable for *kares*!

This is consistent with *Chazal's* famous dictum: The letters of *chametz* and *matzoh* are the same except for the *"ches"* of *chametz* and the *"hay"* of *matzo*h. What difference is there between a *"ches"* and a *"hay"*? One little line. One more minute! That minute makes the difference between *chametz* and *matzoh*. That minute determines spiritual success or its unfortunate counterpart.

The *Midrash, Toras Kohanim*, expresses a similar idea. The *pasuk* in *Vayikra 20:25, 26* reads, *"You shall therefore separate between the clean beast and the unclean and between the unclean fowl and the clean... And I have set you apart from the nations that you should be Mine."* *Chazal* attribute the juxtaposition of the *pesukim* to the relationship between the two "separations." If we distinguish between the clean and unclean animal, between the kosher and non-kosher, between the animal whose two *simanim*, vital organs, foodpipe and windpipe have had the majority of their width ritually slaughtered, Hashem will take us to Him. For the *shechitah* of an animal to be considered kosher, it is necessary that the majority of both the foodpipe and the windpipe are properly slaughtered. Imagine, the amount necessary to make the *shechitah* kosher is nothing more than a *ma'shehu*, a tiny drop, insignificant in size but greatly significant in its impact. That tiny hairbreadth distinguished *Bnei Yisrael* from the Egyptians. That minuscule amount delineates between *matzoh* and *chametz*.

On the night of *Pesach* thousands of years ago, Hashem chose us over the Egyptians as He has chosen us above all the nations of the world to be His *am segulah*, treasured nation. This selection separates us from all the rest. We must continue to strive to earn this distinction.

Matzoh – Pesach's Signature Food

מצה זו שאנו אוכלים על שום מה? על שום שלא הספיק בצקם של אבותינו להחמיץ עד שנגלה עליהם מלך מלכי המלכים הקב"ה וגאלם.

Why do we eat this matzoh? It is because the dough of our fathers did not have time to ferment before the King of Kings, the Holy One, blessed is He, revealed Himself to them and redeemed them.

*T*he *Rambam* writes that *matzoh* is a reminder of our bondage, representing the *lechem oni*, bread of affliction, which our ancestors ate while they were slaves in Egypt. It also commemorates the speed with which Hashem redeemed them. They had no time to bake bread to take with them for this journey. They were, consequently, forced to make *matzos* in order to avoid the delay inherent in preparing leavened bread.

Horav S.R. Hirsch, z"l, views these two reasons as complementary to one another. It is significant to note that *Bnei Yisrael* played no role in their own liberation. They did not fight; they could not even leave their homes. They simply waited for their freedom. What did they do to earn their freedom? What rendered them worthy of liberation? They attained their freedom through their devotion to Hashem. By sacrificing the god of the Egyptians as the *Korban Pesach*, they demonstrated their total subservience to the Almighty. Yet, they still took no part in their own deliverance. They did not eat the *matzoh*, which represented their slavery, until the very last moments. During that final moment of redemption, when they were "summoned" to leave, they grabbed whatever food they had and left. They had no bread because they had no time to prepare it. Hence, the *matzoh*, the unleavened, incomplete bread, serves as eternal testimony of the Divine nature of *Yetzias Mitzrayim*. The *matzoh* is a tribute to the fact that it was Hashem—only Hashem—Who effected our release. To paraphrase *Horav Hirsch,* "How could a people, incapable of preparing itself with proper provisions for such a great journey, think that they were instrumental in obtaining their own freedom?"

The *Bnei Yissaschar* cites the *Zohar Ha'kadosh* who expresses a similar view. *Matzoh* is referred to as מיכלא דמהימנותא, the food of trust (in Hashem). Dough which has a leavening agent in it continues to rise on its own, even after it has been kneaded. Unleavened dough has no power of its own. It rises only when man kneads it. The inert quality of unleavened dough is symbolic of our liberation. We did nothing to effect our freedom. It was the exclusive work of Hashem. During the Festival of Freedom, we eat the food that best describes Hashem's Hand in our deliverance.

Horav Eli Munk, z"l, suggests another reason that *matzoh* is an ideal symbol for our Festival of Freedom. We are enjoined to rid ourselves of *chametz*, leaven, which is *matzoh's* counterpart. Leaven initiates fermentation by decomposing the dough. In this process, a pure, static, natural material is subjected to the work of man who kneads, molds, and shapes it to fit his own taste. This represents man's mastery over nature. Likewise in the spiritual dimension, the *yetzer hora*, evil inclination, causes the human soul to ferment through its "ability" to decompose the soul's natural purity by provoking it to oppose the forces of good. The *yetzer hora* creates discord within the human personality in the same manner that leaven distorts the wholesomeness of the flour and water. Indeed, as *Horav Munk* notes, the numerical equivalent of חמץ, leaven, is 138, the same number as פגימה, blemish/defect.

As *Pesach* approaches, we are adjured to search for and destroy all *chametz*. This requirement imbues the Festival of Freedom, the holiday commemorating our people's birth as a nation, with a feeling of complete moral, physical, and national renewal. As we rid our homes of *chametz*, we must similarly rid ourselves of any vestige of envy and hatred. This festival is consistent with the season of *Aviv*, Spring—the time of nature's renewal.

With this in mind, it is truly appropriate that the "national" food for this holiday is *matzoh*. It represents our return to national purity. Our inauguration as the nation of Hashem is characterized by purity and integrity. After the seven-day festival, we return to our usual eating patterns epitomized by leavened bread. Our abstinence from *chametz* at the beginning of the year inspires us to be resolute in ridding ourselves of the vestiges of evil which plague us. Hence, the taste of *matzoh* remains with us all year long.

A Paradox – Pesach and Tisha B'Av

מרור זה שאנו אוכלים של שום מה?

Marror – Why do we eat this bitter herb?

*T*he night of the first *Seder* occurs on the same day of the week as *Tisha B'Av* of that year. On the night that we rejoice in celebration over our good fortune in being redeemed from Egypt, we are to remember *Tisha B'Av*, the day of the year set aside for the commemoration of the *churban*, the day of the destruction of our *Batei Mikdash*. Why is it necessary to integrate misery with joy? Are we not taught that everything has its own time and place? *Horav Mordechai Gifter, shlita*, suggests two reasons for this. First, at the moment of heightened spiritual joy, when we experience the freedom from bondage and the accompanying *kedushah*, holiness, it is incumbent to reflect simultaneously upon the bitterness of exile. Thus, we will appreciate our present condition all the more.

We note a second – more profound — aspect to this reflection. We must realize that until the final moment of the *geulah*, freedom, we were *still* tottering at the brink of destruction. The *yetzer hora*, evil inclination, who challenges us every step of the way works "timelessly" to bring about our destruction. The source of *churban* is *there* waiting to grasp hold of us, preventing our liberation, hindering our triumph. That same night that resulted in "*matzoh*", freedom and joy, could just have easily been transformed into "*marror*," bitterness and destruction.

One must always realize that the *derech aliyah*, road to spiritual ascendancy, is fraught with the blandishments of the *yetzer hora* every step of the way. We cannot falter, even for a moment, or the fangs of the *yetzer hora* grab hold, pulling us down to ruin and oblivion.

Rather than focusing upon destruction as the catalyst for appreciating freedom and joy, we suggest an alternative approach. In order to accurately assess the magnitude of the loss of an object, one must first appreciate that which he had in his possession. Only after one is sensitive to the vibrancy and beauty of the *Bais Hamikdash* service can he heighten his awareness of the meaning of its destruction.

Horav Levi Yitzchok Horowitz, shlita, the Bostoner *Rebbe*, distinguishes between two forms of remembrance which *Chazal* have
instituted: *zeicher l'churban* and *zeicher l'Mikdash*. The latter recalls
the vibrancy and sanctity that permeated the *Bais Hamikdash*, while
the former commemorates the destruction of the *Bais Hamikdash*. The
zeicher l'churban is more of a passive approach to remembrance. We
are to refrain from participating in unbridled joy. Upon decorating
our homes, we leave a small corner unfinished as a reminder that as
long as the *Bais Hamikdash* is destroyed, our lives are no longer complete. When we prepare a meal, we leave one condiment off the table;
ashes are placed upon the heads of a *chasan* and *kallah*, all *zeicher
l'churban*. In regard to *zeicher l'Mikdash*, however, the emphasis is
upon the positive. We recall the *Bais Hamikdash* and the Judaism that
flourished during its tenure.

Consequently, the Jew mourns in an unusual, almost paradoxical,
way. The same Jew who rises in middle of the night to cry as he recites
Tikkun Chatzos, the prayer commemorating the destruction of the *Bais
Hamikdash*, also dances joyfully with the *lulav* and *esrog* on *Sukkos* –
all to memorialize the *Bais Hamikdash*. He cries in remembrance, and
he dances and sings in remembrance. The Jewish family, who sits on
the floor *erev Tisha B'Av* mournfully eating eggs and ashes, several
months later will sit down to a table bedecked in finery in order to eat
a scrumptious meal on *Pesach*. They eat *matzoh* and *marror wrapped*
together to commemorate the *Mikdash*. Indeed, the entire *Seder* is a
paradox! The white *kittel* is the garment that nobility wears, it is also
used as shrouds for the dead. The *marror* commemorates the bitterness and affliction, while the *matzoh* is the symbol of freedom.

We do not minimize our happiness by remembering the destruction, because our tears for the *Bais Hamikdash* are not relevant to the
Seder. We remember the *Bais Hamikdash* in a positive, constructive
mode. Our entire festival cycle recalls the service in the *Bais
Hamikdash* in all its splendor. We do not recall destruction. We remember the functioning of the *Bais Hamikdash*. The lesson is simple:
The Jew does not constantly focus upon the loss and devastation. To
do so would be counterproductive to Judaism, in addition to emotionally draining for the individual. The proper approach towards

venerating the past is to mourn with dignity at the appropriate times and to honor in a positive, resolute manner at other times.

The *Seder* night is a night of education. It is a night in which we raise our awareness regarding joy, freedom, and hope, as well as — in contrast — servitude, persecution and depression. The Jewish calendar is filled with times which commemorate both. How do we relate to this moment? How do we express ourselves during these times? On the *Seder* night we wrap together the *matzoh* of freedom and the *marror* of affliction to teach us that they go hand in hand for the Jew. We cannot mourn a destruction unless we are aware of what we have lost. We are obligated to remember our loss in a positive, active manner. This way we will merit to bring it all back – במהרה בימינו – one day soon!

Marror's Enigma

וימררו את חייהם בעבדה קשה ... את כל עבדתם אשר עבדו בהם בפרך.
They embittered their lives with hard labor ... whatever labor they made them perform was with crushing harshness.

We memorialize the bitterness of Egypt, the harsh labor and persecution with the *marror*, bitter herbs, which we eat on *Pesach* night. *Chazal* teach us that while there are a number of vegetables that are suitable for the *mitzvah* of *marror*, leaf lettuce is preferable. Among the vegetables, leaf lettuce serves as the best symbol of the type of labor to which the Egyptians subjected the Jewish people. At first, the Egyptians convinced the Jews to work *with* them. Later on, they embittered their lives with harsh labor. At first, the lettuce seems almost sweet to the palate. Its bitter taste is only manifest later. This reason for preferring leaf lettuce to *marror* is enigmatic. We seek to remember the bitterness of the Egyptian exile. Yet, we eat a vegetable that recalls the "sweet" beginning of our bondage. Is the memory bitter or sweet?

Horav Yosef Zundel Salant, z"l, notes two forms of suffering. One type of suffering is inflicted upon a person by others. This is undoubtedly difficult to bear, but it is more tolerable than the pain and suffering that is self-inflicted, when one has become complicitous in creating his own misery. Had the Egyptians originally conscripted the Jews into slave labor without pretext, the Jews might have been able to accept the concept of bondage, as painful as it would have been. The circumstances preceding the Egyptian slavery were different. The Jews had never considered that their "good" friends and neighbors would actually enslave them. The sweetness compounded the bitterness, for the Jews had contributed to bringing the misery upon themselves.

Perhaps this is the idea behind the custom of dipping the *marror* into the sweet *charoses*. We recall the bitterness with which we lived as a result of accepting the Egyptian blandishments. The Egyptians smiled at us, making us feel good. Our own insecurity led to our ultimate torment. If we would only learn a lesson from the message of the *marror*, it might prevent other tragedies from occurring—even in our own time.

Miracles Eternal

בכל דור ודור חייב אדם לראות את עצמו כאלו הוא יצא ממצרים.
In every generation it is man's duty to regard himself
as though he (personally) had come out of Egypt.

𝓗orav Mordechai Gifter, shlita, explains that all the events which occurred to *Am Yisrael* were not singular, transitory events that were meant to be immediately forgotten. Every miracle, every incident bespeaks *nitzchiyus*, eternity. The events are eternalized in such a manner that when that date on the calendar arrives, a Jew must relate to "then" as if it were "now." Indeed, as the *Baal Haggadah* says, one must *"regard himself as though he came out of Egypt."* This is not an event of the past; it is occurring in the present. Consequently, one is obligated to recite *Hallel* — even at night — since it is viewed as if the miracle occurred to him personally.

In a similar vein, *Horav Eliyahu E. Dessler, z"l,* observes that time is not a line that passes above us, but rather a circle through which we travel. Periodically, we *return* to those events which have been eternalized as a result of the spiritual values with which they have been suffused. During these unique periods, one has the opportunity to interface with the experiences which have consecrated these moments in time. Thus, at the specific time of the year when we remember *Zman Cheiruseinu*, time of our liberation, we are infused with the spiritual concepts that highlight that moment in time. We are inspired by the *kedushah*, holiness, of the moment, we are elevated by the experiences as we relive *Yetzias Metzrayim*.

A Time for Action

היתה יהודה לקדשו ישראל ממשלותיו

Yehudah became His Sanctuary, Yisrael His dominion.

The *Mechilta* describes the scenario and the dialogue that took place among the tribes prior to the splitting of the Sea. *Bnei Yisrael* were standing by the shores of the Red Sea; the Egyptian army was literally breathing down their necks. Suddenly, they began to argue about who should go into the water first. Each tribe vied for the opportunity to enter the Red Sea first. During the negotiations, Nachshon *ben* Aminadav, of the tribe of Yehudah, jumped into the threatening waters. The tribe of Yehudah was indeed lauded for this singular act of devotion, as it is stated in *Tehillim 114*, *"Yehudah became His Sanctuary, Yisrael His dominion."* Indeed, for his decisiveness and alacrity in taking the first plunge, Yehudah was crowned as king over *Bnei Yisrael*. Why should Yehudah receive all of the acclaim? His unique act notwithstanding, the members of each of the tribes were *also* willing to jump into the water!

We may suggest the following: Meetings are essential, and a consensus of opinion is necessary. When *Klal Yisrael* was trapped between the forbidding waters of the Red Sea and the approaching Egyptian Army, it was not the time to make speeches and convene meetings. It was a time for action and commitment, not rhetoric and hyperbole. All too often when action on behalf of a *Torah* cause is mandated, be it response to organizational, communal, or individual needs, we become constrained by meetings, speeches and votes. The problem at hand festers and, in most cases, grows out of proportion. We must recognize that Hashem determined that the *Bais Hamikdash* was to be built in

Yehudah's portion of the land as a result of his commitment to action and practice. Similarly, *Klal Yisrael* will grow vibrantly only if we put our faith and commitment into active participation and practice.

Perceiving Nature's Miracles

The Sea saw and fled.   הים ראה וינס

ℬnei Yisrael were saved from certain death when the waters of the Red Sea "saw and fled," as they split before the Jews. What happened, however, after it was "all over," and *Bnei Yisrael* had passed safely through the sea? The *Torah* tells us in *Shemos 14:26* that Moshe was commanded to *"stretch out your hand over the sea, that the waters may come back."*

It seemed unnecessary for Moshe to have stretched out his hand across the waters in order to return the sea to its natural position. Once the purpose of the miracle had been fulfilled and its effect confirmed, would the waters not have "returned" to their original state on "their own"? *Horav Mordechai Gifter, shlita,* derives a remarkable insight from this *pasuk*. We have become so accustomed to believing in the concept of "nature" that we fail to realize that *teva*, nature is actually *neis*, miracle. The natural order of creation and the functioning of the world has license to exist *only* as a result of the will of Hashem. When Hashem expressed His desire that the waters separate, that reality immediately became the new order of "nature." Life does not simply return to "business as usual" after the miracle has ended. In order for the Sea to have reverted to its original state – its pre-miracle standard – another miracle was needed. Indeed, it is our goal to be able to perceive the constant miracles in what we consider to be "routine" nature.

"Hand It" Over

הים ראה וינס הירדן יסב לאחור

The Sea saw and fled; the Jordan turned backward.

𝒯he *Midrash*, cited by the *Daas Zekeinim*, comments that when *Bnei Yisrael* approached the Red Sea, menacing waters confronted them. No hope seemed to be in sight. The Angel Gavriel came forth and declared, "Let the waters in front of *Bnei Yisrael* move away in deference to the nation who perform the *bris milah*. The waters which are to the right of *Bnei Yisrael* should likewise defer to the nation that accepted the *Torah* from Hashem's "right Hand." The waters to the left should submit to the nation that puts *tefillin* on the left arm, and the waters behind them should move away before those that don the *tallis* and cast the *tzitzis* over their shoulders."

The *z'chus*, merit, of these *mitzvos* rendered *Bnei Yisrael* worthy of *Krias Yam Suf*, the splitting of the Red Sea. These *mitzvos*, however, seem to have little in common with one another. Although *tefillin*, *bris milah*, and *tzitzis/tallis* are all related to the body, *Kabbolas ha'Torah* from Hashem's "right Hand" is not an act which we perform with our body. Our right hand did not receive the *Torah*; rather, it was Hashem's "right Hand" that gave it to us! What, then, is the parallel between *Torah* study and the other three *mitzvos*?

We suggest that a profound lesson can be inferred from here. The three *mitzvos* mentioned herein — in fact all *mitzvos* — are primarily active in nature. This means that one performs them on his own; the element of instruction is not an integral component in the framework of the *mitzvah*. *Torah* study, on the other hand, is unique in the fact that it must be transmitted by a *rebbe*, *Torah* teacher.

Torah is passed down from teacher to student in a chain of transmission from *Har Sinai* until this very day. Moshe received the *Torah* from Hashem *Yisborach* and "handed it over" to Yehoshua, who, in turn, handed it over to the next generation. Similarly, every *Torah* teacher transmits the *Torah* to his student. This method of *Torah* study is an integral part of the *mitzvah* of *limud ha'Torah*. One does not study on his own; he receives the *Torah* insights from his *rebbe*, and reviews them until they become a part of his consciousness. Only then is he able to transmit to others that which he absorbed within himself. Moshe received the *Torah* and "handed it" over to Yehoshua. He did not "give it" over. To give something over implies a transfer of ownership. One gives over what one possesses. To hand or turn over means to transfer the message as is — preserved in its entirety. The trust of every *rebbe* in *Klal Yisrael* from the time of Moshe *Rabbeinu* is to see to it that the *Torah* in its immutable form is transmitted through the generations, as pristine and untampered as it came to us at Sinai.

Consequently, it is the *receiving* of the *Torah from* Hashem's "right Hand" that characterizes the significance of the *mitzvah*. *Limud ha'Torah* is an active *mitzvah* which is fulfilled through the passive reception of a *talmid* from his *rebbe*.

Three Exiles – One Weapon

ישראל בטח בד' עזרם ומגנם הוא, בית אהרן בטחו בד' ...
יראי בד' בטחו בד' ...

Yisrael, trust in Hashem! He is their help and shield! House of Aharon, trust in Hashem! ... You who revere Hashem, trust in Hashem ...

The *Ozrover Rebbe, z"l*, posits that this *pasuk* alludes to the three forms of *galus*, exile. The first form of exile is the one with which we are all familiar, the exile of the Jews among the nations. The second exile is the one in which the *tzaddik*, righteous Jew, the upstanding *Torah* scholar, is relegated to live among and endure those who disparage the *Torah* and its disseminators. The third exile is a personal exile that we endure, the exile of man against his *yetzer hora*, evil inclination. Through all these exiles, we are encouraged to trust in Hashem, maintaining our fortitude, so that we will triumph over the challenges.

"*Yisrael b'tach b'Hashem*" refers to the most common *galus*, the Jew as a stranger in a non-Jewish world. *Bitachon*, trust in the Almighty, will help him to overcome the trials and tribulations with which he is confronted.

"*Bais Aharon bitchu b'Hashem*" addresses the second and no less significant trying situation, the torment experienced among those who have distanced themselves from the *Torah* and everything it represents. From the first national leader, Moshe *Rabbeinu*, to those who shepherd our nation in contemporary times, the disseminators of *Torah* and those who devote their lives to its mastery have been subjected to a constant battle. They have been humiliated and scorned, but have continued to grow by placing their trust in Hashem.

The *pasuk*, "*Yirei Hashem bitchu b'Hashem*" refers to the last *galus*, the exile braved by the intensely G-d fearing Jew. Everyone must overcome his personal confrontation with the *yetzer hora*. How many, however, view this as suffering, as a *galus ruchni*, a spiritual exile? The *tzaddik* is the unique individual, whose devotion to Hashem is exemplary. His *yiraas Shomayim*, fear of Heaven, is the touchstone of his character. He truly suffers as he challenges his *yetzer hora*. He, too, will triumph as he places his faith in Hashem.

Bringing Heaven to Earth

השמים שמים לד׳ והארץ נתן לבני אדם

The heaven is Hashem's heaven, but He has given the earth to mankind.

Horav Eliyahu Lopian, z"l, explains that Hashem has granted man the ability to bring heaven down to earth by sanctifying himself and that which is around him. Man has been able to bring sanctity to earth in certain realms. The other areas that have been consecrated by his endeavor remain that way forever. Hence, *Har Ha'Moriah*, the mountain upon which Yitzchak *Avinu* was bound, prepared to be offered as a sacrifice to Hashem, remains eternally holy. The *Bais Hamikdash* was built on this particular site, because of the enormous amount of *kedushah* absorbed therein. Indeed, even after the destruction of the *Batei Mikdash*, the holiness of the site is retained. In contrast is *Har Sinai,* upon which Hashem descended to give the *Torah* to us. Its *kedushah* departed with the departure of the *Shechinah*. Since this act of sanctification was not initiated by man, it does not maintain a lasting presence in man's domain, the earth.

Klal Yisrael – Cornerstone of the World

אבן מאסו הבונים היתה לראש פנה

The stone which the builders rejected has become the cornerstone.

"Even," the cornerstone, refers to David Ha'Melech who was passed over by his own father and brothers. Indeed, when Shmuel Ha'Navi proclaimed that one of Yishai's (David's father's) sons was to be anointed as king over *Am Yisrael*, no one ever glanced at David. No one ever dreamed that this simple, virtuous shepherd would one day tend Hashem's flock, *Klal Yisrael*. *Chazal* compare *Klal Yisrael* to the *"even,"* the cornerstone of the world. Scorned by the nations, who do not realize that their very own existence is intricately bound up with that of *Klal Yisrael*, we endure as the cornerstone of the world's existence. We have contributed virtue, spirituality and morals to a world replete with decadence and depravity. Yet, we are often disparaged as lowly parasites sponging off the world. The nations have treated us as beggars and pariahs, demeaned our contributions, and rejected our advice. With the advent of *Moshiach tzidkeinu*, the nations of the world will finally see and come to realize that we truly are the cornerstone of the world.

That is the simple interpretation which the commentators expound. *Horav Nissan Alpert, z'l,* takes a more homiletic approach towards understanding this *pasuk*. He asks who the builders are and what stone are they rejecting. In every generation, there are those who arise with a collection of "new" ideas and values, prepared to rebuild society and the world as we know it. They seek to heal the world of its ills, mend society of its broken fences, and save humanity from its past errors. Every new group has one thing in common with its predecessors — destruction. They feel that they must first literally destroy the foundation laid down before them by the previous generation: Nothing that has been accomplished before them was positive. The new generation builds upon destruction; they create upon the ruins of others; they save a world only after they have devastated and rejected everything that has existed before them. This goes on without fail every time a new ideal is about to be presented. First, demolish the old; then, build anew. They sever the relationship between father and son, between the past generation and the present. They disparage their parents' way of life; they scorn their "antiquated" culture. The end result is usually the same, building upon that which you have first destroyed. Ultimately they have lost sight of something critically important: It is unnecessary to destroy the old, there is so much value in the past – build upon it, don't destroy it.

This is David *Ha'Melech's* message: The stone of *Yisrael*, the אבן which is a mnemonic for אב and בן, father and son, refers to the relationship between parents and children, past generations and the present. That which others have scorned will be the cornerstone for building our future. Only through our connection with the past will we be able to build a lasting future.

פנינים הגדה של פסח
The Peninim
HAGGADAH

Question
&
Answer Section

When should one begin studying the laws pertaining to *Pesach*?

A. Thirty days before *Pesach*.

 What is *maos chittim*?

A. *Maos chittim* literally means "wheat money," or money used for purchasing wheat to be distributed to the poor in accordance with their needs for *Pesach*. We ensure that the poor are also provided with wine, meat, and fish so that they can enjoy the Festival of Freedom *(Pesach)* as "free" people.

 Why is *maos chittim* such an important custom?

A. One cannot appreciate the full meaning of freedom as long as he is aware that his neighbor does not have anything to eat. When he recites in the *Haggadah*, *Kol dichfin yesei v'yeichol*, "let those who are hungry come in and eat", he must be sincere. This can only be true if he has made sure that others have been provided for.

 Why is it a greater *mitzvah* to give *tzedakah* prior to *Pesach* than during other times of the year?

A. *Matzoh* is much more expensive than *chametz*. We are therefore concerned that a poor person will forgo eating *matzoh* and save his money for food, even if it may be *chametz*.

 What special name is given to the *Shabbos* before *Pesach*?

A. *Shabbos Ha'gadol*.

Why is this *Shabbos* given this name?

A. *Bnei Yisrael* were told to take lambs in preparation for the *Korban Pesach.* When the Egyptians saw them taking these lambs on *Shabbos*, the day of rest, they were surprised and questioned *Bnei Yisrael's* behavior. When the Jews responded that they were preparing these animals to be used for a sacrifice, the Egyptians were shocked. After all, the sheep was their god. Hashem made a miracle, and *Bnei Yisrael* were saved from certain catastrophe in their confrontation with the Egyptians. In remembrance of this great miracle which occurred on *Shabbos,* the tenth of *Nissan,* we call this *Shabbos* "*Shabbos Ha'gadol,*" the Great *Shabbos.*

 We have a custom to read from the *Haggadah* after *Minchah* on *Shabbos Ha'gadol.*
a) What do we read? b) and why?

A. a) לכפר על כל עונותינו until עבדים היינו.

b) The redemption began on *Shabbos.* Also, reading the *Haggadah* familiarizes children with its contents. Additionately, it is somewhat of a "rehearsal" for the *Seder.*

 What else occurred on the tenth of *Nissan?*

A. Miriam *Ha'Neviyah* died, and *Bnei Yisrael* were deprived of the benefits of her well. [*Bnei Yisrael* had a well in the desert in Miriam's merit. *(Taanis* 9a).] A year later *Bnei Yisrael* crossed the Jordan River on their way into *Eretz Yisrael.*

Q **a) What *tefillah* is omitted during *Nissan*?**
b) Why?

A. a) *Tachanun.*

b) The twelve *Nesiim* (tribal leaders) each offered a sacrifice in honor of the *Chanukas Ha'Mishkan*. Hence, the first twelve days of *Nissan* were considered *Yomim Tovim*. In addition, *Erev Pesach*, the *Yom Tov* itself, and *Isru Chag* are days when *Tachanun* is not recited. Since *Tachanun* is not recited for so many days of the month, it is omitted the entire month.

Q **Which *mitzvah* concerning *Pesach* is performed prior to the *Yom Tov*?**

The removal of the *chametz*, leavened food products.

Q **How soon before *Pesach* may one make *bedikas chametz*, the search for *chametz*?**

A. As early as thirty days before *Pesach*. In order that the *mitzvah* have greater significance in our eyes *Chazal* have set aside the eve of the 14th of *Nissan* as the time for *bedikas chametz*.

Q **When should the search for the *chametz* begin?**

A. On the 14th of *Nissan*, as soon after nightfall as possible.

Q **If one nullifies the *chametz* in his possession in his mind, is it sufficient?**

A. According to the *Torah* it is sufficient to make *bitul*, annulment. *Chazal*, however, have decreed that one must search for and destroy the *chametz*.

Why is it necessary to do both, *bedikah* and *bitul*?

A. First, not all people perform the act of annulment with the same level of sincerity. *Chazal* therefore felt it would be best to search for and remove the *chametz* prior to its annulment. Second, since people are accustomed to eat *chametz* all year round, they might forget the prohibition if they find some *chametz* in their homes on *Pesach*. Consequently, to circumvent any problems, one should make a *bedikah* and afterwards *bitul*.

What type of light should one use for *bedikas chametz*?

A. One should use a candle with which he can search in places such as cracks and crevices which are not readily visible during the light of the day.

What is another reason why *Chazal* instituted *bedikas chametz* at night?

A. Most people are home at night.

May one do work or eat a meal before *bedikas chametz*?

A. No. One is forbidden to do work from half an hour before nightfall. One should also not sit down to eat a meal during this time.

What *brachah* does one make prior to *bedikas chametz*?

A. אשר קדשנו במצותיו וצונו על בעור חמץ

Why does he not say על בדיקת חמץ ?

A. The *bedikah* is actually the beginning of the *mitzvah* of *biur chametz*, burning the *chametz*.

 What follows the *biur chametz*?

A. *Bitul chametz* — we nullify ownership over the *chametz* in our possession.

 Why then is there not a *brachah* recited על בטול חמץ ?

A. *Bitul chametz* is a *mitzvah* which is performed in one's heart and mind. A *brachah* is not recited on such a *mitzvah*.

 Why do we not recite a *Shehechiyanu* on *bedikas chametz*?

A. The *bedikah* is part of the *Yom Tov*. When we say *Shehechiyanu* during *Kiddush* on the first night, it encompasses all the *mitzvos* connected with *Pesach*. Moreover, this *brachah* is recited only during a time of joy, when one derives physical benefit from the *mitzvah*. When we search for *chametz*, however, we are full of anguish at having to rid ourselves of the *chametz*.

 What should be done prior to the search to ensure that all the *chametz* is found?

A. Ten small pieces of *chametz* should be scattered around the house to be found during the *bedikah*, and the search for these ten pieces will thus ensure the finding of any remaining *chametz*.

What is the significance of the ten pieces?

A. The decree which Haman wrote to destroy the Jews was written on the 13th of *Nissan* . His ten sons served as scribes for issuing the decree. The Jewish people compensated for these ten scribes by accepting upon themselves the placement of ten pieces of bread, symbolizing their intention to eradicate the evil within themselves through the search and removal of *chametz*. (Haman was executed three days later , on the second day of *Pesach*.) Also, the ten pieces allude to the ten plagues Hashem inflicted upon Egypt.

On *Erev Pesach*, when does one make *bitul*, before burning the *chametz* or afterwards?

A. Afterwards.

Why is the *Kol Chamira*, the text for the *bitul chametz*, recited in Aramaic?

A. Firstly, it was the spoken language at the time that *Chazal* instituted the decree. Secondly, in an effort to avoid disrespect for bread, the staff of life, *Chazal* instituted a language which is not accessible to the *shei-dim*, demons.

If one either forgot or did not have the opportunity to search for the *chametz* on the night of the 14th, what should he do?

A. He should make *bedikas chametz* on the following day with a candle. He should also recite the *brachah*.

What actually is *chametz*?

A. Any flour made of wheat, spelt, barley, rye, or oats which is mixed with water and allowed to ferment before being baked is included in the definition of *chametz*.

 What amount of time is allotted for the fermentation process?

A. *Chazal* have determined that if eighteen minutes have elapsed from the time of adding the water to the flour and nothing has been done to the mixture, then it is definitely *chametz*.

 What is *ta'aruvas chametz*?

A. This refers to a mixture of *chametz* with other food.

 What is *chametz nukshah*?

A. This refers to something which is not completely *chametz*, such as paste made from flour, or *chametz* which has never been in a state really fit for human consumption. However, once it has been considered a food, it retains this status until it is no longer fit for a dog to eat.

 May *chametz nukshah* be kept in one's possession during *Pesach*?

A. Although the *Torah* does not prohibit it, *Chazal* have decreed that it must be destroyed.

 How large an amount of *chametz* is forbidden to be eaten on *Pesach*?

A. *Chametz* is *asur b'mashehu*: even the smallest particle is forbidden. In the event that a minute quantity of *chametz* has been mixed with a much greater amount of permissible food, the entire quantity is forbidden. This *halachah* applies only during *Pesach*. If, however, this minute quantity has been mixed in before *Pesach*, when *chametz* is still in its permissible state, it becomes *batel b'shishim*, neutralized by sixty times its amount, providing that the *chametz* is completely dissolved and is no longer detectable.

What is the meaning of *matzoh shmurah*?

A. Guarded *matzoh*. Ordinary *matzoh* is watched from the time that the wheat is ground, in order to ensure that it does not come in contact with anything that can make it *chametz*. Every precaution is taken regarding the flour, water, and utensils used for making the *matzoh*. *Matzoh shmurah* is *matzoh* that was guarded from the time that the wheat was harvested. Many people will use *matzoh shmurah* for the first two nights of *Pesach*, when eating *matzoh* is a positive command.

What type of water is used for making *matzoh*?

A. The water must have stood overnight after being drawn from a river or a well. It must remain in a vessel completely removed from the source of water for twelve hours.

What is this water called?

A. *Mayim she'lanu*, water that has stood overnight.

Why is *matzoh* very thin?

A. In order for it to be called *lechem oni*, bread of affliction.

What is *matzoh nefuchah*?

A. *Matzoh* that is bent or folded over. We forbid this type of *matzoh*, since it cannot be baked properly.

Q What is *matzoh nefuchah?*

A. Blownup *matzoh*. The *matzoh* is either blown up in the middle, or the bottom part is separated from the top part of the *matzoh*. The heat does not penetrate these spots, so the *matzoh* cannot be baked properly, therefore it is not permissible.

Q What are *kitniyos?*

A. Legumes, or anything from the rice or bean family. The prevalent custom among Ashkenazic Jews is to refrain from eating these species on *Pesach*. The reason is that some of these vegetables are ground into a type of flour suitable for making bread. If one were to use foods made from this type of "flour" on *Pesach* he might be inclined to downplay the laws of *chametz*. Furthermore, it used to be common to mix other grains with rice. Thus, it was felt that it would be easier to refrain from eating rice than to guard the rice from being mixed with other grains.

Q What special features are associated with *Erev Pesach?*

A. 1) *Bechorim* fast on *Erev Pesach*.

2) It was the first day of the three-day fast decreed by Mordechai and Esther in Shushan.

3) It is a day set aside for fasting by pious people.

4) In *Eretz Yisrael* all leftover *maasros'* (tithes) are disposed of on *Erev Pesach* of the former *Shmittah* year (Sabbatical year) and on *Erev Pesach* of the *Shmittah* year itself. This is referred to as *biur ha'maasros*.

5) It is the day that Yaakov *Avinu* was blessed.

6) David *Ha'melech* would never go out to war on *Erev Pesach*, since this was a day reserved for blessing.

7) *Chametz* is disposed of in the morning.

Why do the firstborn males fast on *Erev Pesach*?

A. It is in remembrance of the fact that the firstborn Jews were spared from death during *Makas Bechoros*, the plague of the smiting of the firstborn.

Were the firstborn sons of Egypt smitten on *Erev Pesach*?

A. No. They were killed on *Pesach* night. We do not, however, fast on *Yom Tov*.

Why do most *bechorim* participate in a *siyum* on *Erev Pesach*?

A. The fast is generally treated with leniency. Subsequently, if there is a *seudas mitzvah*, such as a *siyum* the *bechor* participates in the *siyum*.

What is a *Taanis Chasidim*?

A. Pious people are accustomed to fast on *Erev Pesach* even if they are not *bechorim*. They want to eat *matzoh* at the *Seder* with the proper appetite. Also, this is the anniversary of the day that Haman issued the decree to kill the Jews.

May one eat *matzoh* on *Erev Pesach*?

A. The type of *matzoh* which one uses to perform the *mitzvah* at the *Seder* may not be eaten all day. Indeed, people have the custom not to eat *matzoh* from *Rosh Chodesh Nissan* until *Pesach* in order to enhance the *mitzvah* of *achilas matzoh*, eating *matzoh*.

Should the *Seder* table be set in any specific manner?

A. Yes. One should place a very nice tablecloth upon the table. The finest silverware and dishes one owns should be used on *Pesach* night. Although ostentation is not a Jewish quality, the "rich" ambiance (general atmosphere) promotes the idea of freedom and joy.

What special garment does the head of the household wear for the *Seder*? Why does he do so?

A. It is customary to wear a plain white *kittel*. One of the reasons stated for this custom is that the dead are clothed in a white *kittel* prior to burial. Amidst the pomp and elegance that are customary on this night, this garment will prevent a person from being arrogant. In addition, *Tisha B'Av*, which commemorates the destruction of the *Batei Mikdash* always occurs on the same day of the week as the first day of *Pesach*. A symbol of mourning is therefore appropriate. For the same reason, many people have the custom at the *Seder* to eat eggs, which are a symbol of mourning. An alternative explanation is that a plain white garment is a symbol of purity. It is what the *Kohen Gadol,* High Priest wore on the holiest day of the year, *Yom Kippur*, when he entered the *Kodshei Kodoshim,* Holy of Holies. When a Jew celebrates the *Seder* he is supposed to feel like the *Kohen Gadol* about to perform the *Avodah,* Temple Service.

Why does the *Seder* night bear this name?

A. *Seder* means "order," referring to the specific manner and sequence in which we perform the *mitzvos* of the evening. The *Maharal* suggests that the *Seder* is a symbol of the miracles and wonders which Hashem did for us. These miracles are the foundation for the miracles granted future generations. These miracles were performed with special intentions and in specific sequence, and all subsequent miracles follow this format. *Pesach* is the forerunner of all other festivals. Every festival of the year is fixed according to the days of *Pesach*. It sets the "*seder*," — the order — for the year.

How many *mitzvos* of the *Torah* pertaining to *Pesach* night are still applicable today?

A. Two. The *mitzvah* of eating *matzoh* and the *mitzvah* of telling the story of the exodus from Egypt.

Is not the *mitzvah* of eating *marror* from the *Torah*?

A. The *marror,* bitter herbs mentioned in the *Torah* were to be eaten together with the *Korban Pesach*. Subsequently, today's obligation has been ordained by *Chazal*.

What other *mitzvah* did *Chazal* ordain?

A. The *Arba Kosos,* four cups of wine.

We have mentioned that there are two *mitzvos* from the *Torah* and two *mitzvos* from *Chazal* that belong exclusively to *Pesach* night. Are there any *customs* that also apply exclusively to this night?

A. Reclining at the table; dipping the *karpas* in salt water, and eating it after washing the hands; dividing the middle *matzoh* and hiding part of it for the end of the meal (*Afikoman*); and eating eggs in salt water are all customs.

Why do we recline during the *Seder*?

A. We recline when we partake of the four cups of wine, the *matzoh*, the *Korech*, and the *Afikoman*. This is the manner in which noble people eat. On this night, all Jews are to conduct themselves as nobility. Another reason is that there is a connection between the Hebrew word "to lean" and the word "to go around". They are both implied in the word "להסב." *Chazal* infer from this that just as Hashem made all *Bnei Yisrael* travel in a circuitous way when He took them out from Egypt, so too must all Jews, regardless of their financial situation, lean at the *Seder* table.

On which side do we recline?

A. One reclines on his left side, while he eats with his right hand. This practice is in effect even if he is left-handed.

Do women recline?

A. The accepted custom is that they do not recline.

During what point in the *Seder* does one recline?

A. It is indeed praiseworthy to recline throughout the entire *Seder*. One is obligated, however, to recline only for the four cups of wine, eating the *matzoh*, and the *Afikoman*.

When does one drink *arba Kosos*, the four cups of wine?

A. (1) for *Kiddush*; (2) for the *mitzvah* of *Haggadah*; (3) *Bircas HaMazon*, when he completes the meal; and (4) to signal the end of *Hallel*.

If one drinks the four cups of wine one after another, does he fulfill the *mitzvah* of *arba kosos*?

A. No.

What color wine should be used for the four cups? Why this color?

A. Red wine, unless its quality is inferior to that of white wine. It brings to mind the blood of the *Bris Milah* and the blood of the *Korban Pesach*. Red wine is a remembrance of the blood that was sprinkled upon the doorposts of Jewish houses which Hashem passed over during *Makas Bechoros*. It also reminds us of the blood of the little children whom Pharaoh slaughtered so that he could bathe in their blood in order to heal himself of leprosy.

 If one cannot afford the four cups of wine, what should he do?

A. Regardless of one's financial status, he must drink the four cups of wine on *Pesach* night. If necessary, one should even sell his clothes in order to purchase the four cups of wine.

 What do the four cups of wine symbolize?

A. The four cups refer to the four stages in the redemption, or the four *"leshonos shel geulah,"* the four expressions of redemption: והוצאתי — "I will *take you out* from the burdens of the yoke of Egypt." Even if we had stayed in Egypt, our yoke of servitude would have been removed. והצלתי — "I will *rescue* you from their slavery." Hashem delivered us from Egypt. וגאלתי — "I will *redeem* you with an outstretched arm." This refers to the wondrous miracles which Hashem wrought against the Egyptians. He confused and crushed our Egyptian oppressors. ולקחתי — "I will *take* you to Me for a nation." This is the greatest aspect of the Redemption. Hashem brought us near Him, thereby granting us spiritual redemption as well.

Another reason, stated by *Chazal,* connects the four cups of wine with the four times Pharaoh's cup is mentioned in *Sefer Bereishis.* Both Yosef and Pharaoh's *sar hamashkim,* chief wine steward were imprisoned together in Egypt. Pharaoh's cups are an allusion to *Bnei Yisrael's* slavery. It is as if Hashem were saying to Yosef, "The slavery begins as the 'cup' is put into the hands of Pharaoh. In the end, however, the cup will be taken from him as your children are redeemed, and they will subsequently thank Hashem by drinking four times from the cup which represents salvation."

The four cups of wine are also likened to the four kingdoms that followed Egypt in enslaving *Klal Yisrael.* Babylon, Persia, Greece, and Rome were synonymous with treachery against our people. Consequently, Hashem will exact retribution from them with four different measures of punishment. The *Abarbanel* suggests that the four cups reflect four periods of redemption for *Klal Yisrael.* The first form of redemption took place when Hashem chose Avraham *Avinu* and his descendants to be the forerunners of His chosen people. The second redemption is with us every day as Hashem sustains us throughout our exile. Despite the various hardships and persecutions to which we have been subjected, we remain a vibrant nation. The fourth redemption awaits us with the advent of *Moshiach Tzidkeinu.*

The *Vilna Gaon* says that the four cups symbolize four worlds: the world we live in, the days of *Moshiach,* the period of *Techias Ha'Meisim,* revival of the dead, and *Olam Ha'bah,* the World To Come. If one carries out the *mitzvos* of the *Seder* in the prescribed manner, with the correct intent and emotion, he is assured of these four worlds.

The *Maharal* sees the four cups of wine as alluding to the four Matriarchs — Sarah, Rivkah, Rachel, and Leah. It was their virtues coupled with those of the *Avos,* Patriarchs through which *Klal Yisrael* was redeemed from Egypt. Indeed, *Chazal* teach us that the three primary *mitzvos* of the *Seder* night — *Pesach, matzoh, and marror* — are observed in the merit of the *Avos.*

Lastly, the *Bnei Yissachar* opines that the four cups serve as a reward for the four virtuous deeds carried out by the Jews in Egypt: They did not change their Hebrew names; they did not change their language from *lashon hakodesh*; they did not commit acts of immorality, and they did not speak *lashon hara* against each other. Although the Jews committed many grave sins, it was these four virtues, which remained as the last barrier to total assimilation, and saved them from spiritual annihilation.

Why is there no specific *brachah* made on the four cups of wine?

A. We do not drink them all at once. Since something might occur that would prevent us from completing the drinking of all four cups, we do not take the chance of making a *brachah* in vain.

Why do we not say the *brachah* of She'asah Nissim during Kiddush?

A. After we complete the *Maggid* portion of the *Seder*, we recite the blessing of "*Asher Ge'alanu*" which includes *she'asah nissim*.

Are there only *four* cups of wine?

A. There is a fifth cup of wine which is referred to as "The Cup of Eliyahu." There is a dispute in the *Talmud* as to the necessity of a fifth cup. Rabbi Tarfon is of the opinion that one should drink a fifth cup in deference to the fifth expression of redemption, "והבאתי," "And I will *bring* you." Rabbi Tarfon's opinion was not accepted. *Chazal* ruled, however, that since we are in doubt regarding the *halachah*, we should pour a fifth cup, but not drink from it. When Eliyahu *Ha'Navi* comes, he will render decisions that will resolve all our doubts. He will likewise clarify this question. Thus, this cup is appropriately called, "the Cup of Eliyahu."

How many *matzos* are placed upon the *Seder* plate?

A. Three.

 What special names are given to these *matzos*?

A. The uppermost one is called "*Kohen*," because the *Kohen* takes precedence in all matters. The middle one is known as "*Levi*," and the bottom one is called "*Yisrael*." The middle one is broken in half during "*Yachatz*." The smaller piece is left in its place and subsequently eaten together with the top *matzoh* for the *mitzvah* of *achilas matzoh*. The large piece is put away to serve as the *Afikoman*. The bottom piece, the one signifying *Yisrael*, is eaten during *Korech*.

 Why do we need three *matzos* for the *Seder* night, when during the year we need only two *challos* for *lechem mishnah*, (double portion of bread)?

A. *Matzoh* is referred to as "*lechem oni*," the "bread of poverty." A poor person never completes his entire meal without putting something aside for the next day, just in case he will not find food. We have to use two whole *matzos* because of the *Yom Tov*, as we do on every *Shabbos*. Therefore, we provide a third *matzoh* so that we can fulfill the requirements of both *lechem oni* and *lechem mishnah*.

 What is symbolized by the specific number of *matzos*?

A. They remind us of the three *Avos*. This teaches us that, although we were slaves, we are heirs to a noble ancestry. We are the children of Avraham, Yitzchok, and Yaakov. The three *matzos* symbolize the three measures of fine flour which Avraham had Sarah bake in honor of the angels who visited them. This took place on *Pesach*. The three *matzos* are also a reminder of the *Korban Pesach* which was offered by the *bechorim*, the firstborn in Egypt. Since this was their first sacrifice, it initiated them as *Kohanim*. Whoever begins to serve as a *Kohen* must offer three kinds of loaves.

What is *karpas*? Why is it used?

A. It is a green vegetable . Any type of green vegetable which is not bitter may be used. It is eaten either cooked or raw after *Kiddush*. A number of reasons are given for its use. First, its use right after *Kiddush* prior to the *Haggadah* and the meal, arouses a child's curiosity, which is one of the goals of the evening. By eating the *karpas* and making the proper blessing on it, we make it unnecessary to recite a "*Borei Pri Ha'Adamah*" on the *marror*. The *marror* is a bitter herb which commemorates the tragic pain and affliction to which we were subjected in Egypt. *Chazal* felt that it would be inappropriate to recite two blessings over the *marror*. Hence, we eat *karpas* to preclude making one of the *brachos* on *marror*. The Hebrew letters of the word כרפס allude to the fact that six hundred thousand Jews were subjected to back-breaking labor. The *"samach"* equals sixty, while the remaining three letters spell out the Hebrew word "פרך," which means "hard labor." Thus sixty times ten thousand Jews slaved for Pharaoh.

What does the *charoses* bring to mind?

A. It is a reminder of the clay and straw which *Bnei Yisrael* used for making bricks.

Must one use horseradish for *marror*?

A. No, there are five vegetables that may be used, but leaf lettuce is the most common. Leaf lettuce has special significance for a number of reasons. It is compared to the type of slavery in Egypt. At first the Egyptians convinced the Jews to work by sweet-talking them. Only later did they make their lives bitter with hard labor. Similarly, at first the lettuce seems almost sweet, but later on its bitter taste becomes apparent. Also the Hebrew word for leaf lettuce is "*chasah*" which is similar to the Hebrew word "*chas*," which means "to have pity." We acknowledge that Hashem took pity on us and liberated us from Egypt.

Q **What are the ingredients that are used for *charoses*, and what is their significance?**

A. Apples, nuts, and wine are the ingredients. Some also add pomegranates, figs, and dates. Apples are a reminder of the apple tree under which Jewish women gave birth. The Jewish men separated from their wives because of slavery. They feared bringing children into a world where they would be slaves. The women gave their husbands courage to persevere and rely on Hashem to redeem them. When the women conceived, they concealed their pregnancies until just prior to giving birth. They would then go out to the fields and give birth under apple trees. The apple tree has a unique characteristic. Only *after* the fruits have emerged do the leaves grow to protect the fruit. The women were communicating a message to Hashem: "We will bear the fruit, we will give birth to the children; now Hashem, You must come to to save them." The other ingredients of the *charoses* are fruits which *Shlomo Ha'Melech* mentions in *Shir Ha'Shirim* that are metaphors for *Klal Yisrael*. In each of the analogies employed by *Shlomo Ha'Melech*, *Klal Yisrael* is praised for their exemplary devotion even when they were embittered. Because of their special behavior their bitterness was turned to sweetness as they were redeemed. On this night, we mark the bittersweet experiences of Egypt. We add red wine to the *charoses* to remind us of the various "bloods" which are connected to the Egyptian experience — the blood of the *Bris Milah*, the blood of the *Korban Pesach* and the blood of the Jewish children who were slaughtered in Egypt.

What do the egg and the shankbone on the *Seder* plate symbolize?

A. These two foods remind us of the two *korbanos* which were offered on *Erev Pesach* and were eaten on Pesach night, the *Korban Pesach* and the *Korban Chagigah*.

What special significance is there to the egg?

A. Being round, an egg has no opening or "no mouth." It symbolizes the hope that the "mouths" of our enemies will be silenced forever.

What is the reason for the custom that we eat boiled eggs in salt water?

A. It is a sign of mourning, because the first night of *Pesach* always coincides with that same day of the week as the night of *Tisha B'Av*, when we commemorate the destruction of the *Bais Ha'Mikdash*, in which we used to offer the *Korban Pesach*. The *Chasam Sofer* gives another reason. With all other foods, the longer they are cooked, the softer they become. The egg, interestingly enough, becomes harder the more it is cooked. *Klal Yisrael* is similar to the egg. The more the gentile nations persecute us, the harder and more determined we become.

Why is the shankbone the preferred choice for remembering the *Korban Pesach*?

A. This bone, "the *Zroa*" (זרוע), symbolizes the outstretched "arm" which Hashem showed the Jews in Egypt.

Q

What is the *Afikoman*?

A. It is part of the middle *matzoh* that was broken at the beginning of the meal and "hidden" until after the meal. It is eaten in commemoration of the *Korban Pesach* that was eaten at the end of the meal. *Afikoman* is the Greek word for dessert. Others suggest that it is in memory of the *matzoh* which was likewise eaten together with the *Korban Pesach*.

Q

When must the *Afikoman* be eaten?

A. It is eaten right before *Bircas Ha'Mazon*. We must make every effort to eat the *Afikoman* before *chatzos*, midnight (according to *halachic* calculations), in memory of the *Korban Pesach* which could not be eaten after that time.

Q

Who authored the *Haggadah*?

A. The *Anshei Knesses Ha'gedolah,* the Men of the Great Assembly.

Q

Which one of the "Four Questions" was changed after the destruction of the second *Bais Ha'Mikdash*?

A. During the time of the *Bais Ha'Mikdash*, the child would ask, "Why is it that on all other nights we may eat meat either roasted, overcooked, or cooked but on this night we eat only roasted meat?" Since we no longer sacrifice the *Korban Pesach* (which was roasted) we substitute another question, namely, "Why is it that on all other nights we eat either sitting or leaning but on this night we may only lean?"

Is there a difference between the *mitzvah* **of remembering the exodus from Egypt that applies throughout the entire year and the one on** *Pesach***?**

A. *HoRav Chaim Brisker, z"l*, points out three differences:

1) On *Pesach*, one must tell over the story of the Exodus to somebody else, or at least, in a question and answer manner.

2) On *Pesach*, he must begin by first relating our shameful aspect and later on to mention our praiseworthy attributes.

3) On *Pesach*, one must also explain the reasons for the various *mitzvos* of the evening.

 Why do we not recite a *brachah* **on the** *mitzvah* **of** *Sippur Yetzias Mitzrayim,* **telling the story of the Exodus ?**

A. 1) One fulfills the obligation for this *brachah* when he says the words, *"Zeicher L'Yetzias Mitzrayim"* during *Kiddush*.

2) It is a *mitzvah* that has no limitations to it. One can either speak very little or expound at length.

The Hebrew Academy of Cleveland

*F*ounded in 1943, the Hebrew Academy of Cleveland is a nationally acclaimed institution educating over 750 children. Its scope encompasses more than transmitting knowledge and inculcating Jewish culture. Our obligation is to continue the glorious chain of our Mesorah and develop a love for Torah, Am Yisrael and Eretz Yisrael.

The growth of the Hebrew Academy — from a basement classroom with a handful of students, to today's magnificent complex with a record enrollment — has been remarkable.

Educational aids and curriculum materials prepared at the Academy are implemented in day schools nationally and across the globe.

The Academy today offers a complete religious and secular educational program from pre-kindergarten through the Philip and Mary Edlis Elementary School, the Jacob Sapirstein Mesivta High School for Boys and the Beatrice Stone Yavne High School for Girls.

Education is provided in a wholesome environment fostering moral and ethical behavior in the Torah-true tradition. Education never stops at the Academy. From early morning Mishnayos class to Voluntary After-School programs, Torah study thrives. Extracurricular projects and recreational activities help foster leadership skills and enhance the students' spirit of Torah.

Another Academy innovation is the Summer Torah Enrichment Program. Camp S.T.E.P. — as it is called — is a full-scale Torah and activities program offering its campers 2 ½ hours of intensive learning each morning, followed by swimming, sports, and exciting trips. A separate Yavne girls Camp S.T.E.P. has developed into a full six-week program, as the Academy continues to serve the community.

The latest addition has been a separate division for 75 immigrant children. Special classes and tutors have been provided to enable them to learn and grow as Torah Jews.

Over 5,000 students have been educated at the Academy, many of whom have assumed leadership positions across the globe. ***Indeed, the Jewish leaders of tomorrow are in the Academy classrooms today.***

פנינים הגדה של פסח
The Peninim
HAGGADAH

פנינים

הגדה

של פסח

A Publication of the
Hebrew Academy of Cleveland

The Peninim
HAGGADAH

*Haggadah Text
with English Translation;
Thought-Provoking Insights
and An Informative Question & Answer Section*

by Rabbi A.L. Scheinbaum

Dedicated in Loving Memory of Our Brother, Brother-in-Law and Uncle

Jeffrey M. Berman

יעקב משה ז"ל בן שמואל הי"ו
נפטר ד' סיון תשנ"ה

He was that rare human being who saw the good in everything and everyone, who continued to smile despite suffering and pain, and who lived for others without demanding anything for himself.

Kindness, warmth and sensitivity were his hallmarks. His *bitachon* in Hashem prevailed through his life's most difficult times; it was the cornerstone of his *Yiddishkeit*. His legacy embodied the qualities of a true *ben Torah*.

יהי זכרו ברוך

Hymie and Marcia Keller
Dovid, Becky, Dov and Shimshon

פנינים הגדה של פסח

The Peninim HAGGADAH

Haggadah Text with English Translation

‎‏ בְּדִיקַת חָמֵץ ‏‎

בָּרוּךְ אַתָּה יְיָ אֱלֹהֵינוּ מֶלֶךְ הָעוֹלָם, אֲשֶׁר קִדְּשָׁנוּ בְּמִצְוֹתָיו, וְצִוָּנוּ עַל בְּעוּר חָמֵץ.

כָּל חֲמִירָא וַחֲמִיעָה דְּאִכָּא בִרְשׁוּתִי דְּלָא חֲמִתֵּהּ וּדְלָא בְעַרְתֵּהּ וּדְלָא יָדַעְנָא לֵיהּ לִבָּטֵל וְלֶהֱוֵי הֶפְקֵר כְּעַפְרָא דְאַרְעָא.

‎‏ בְּעוּר חָמֵץ ‏‎

כָּל חֲמִירָא וַחֲמִיעָה דְּאִכָּא בִרְשׁוּתִי דַּחֲזִתֵּהּ וּדְלָא חֲזִתֵּהּ, דַּחֲמִתֵּהּ, דְּלָא חֲמִתֵּהּ, דְּבִעַרְתֵּהּ וּדְלָא בְעַרְתֵּהּ, לִבָּטֵל וְלֶהֱוֵי הֶפְקֵר כְּעַפְרָא דְאַרְעָא.

‎‏ עֵרוּב תַּבְשִׁילִין ‏‎

בָּרוּךְ אַתָּה יְיָ אֱלֹהֵינוּ מֶלֶךְ הָעוֹלָם, אֲשֶׁר קִדְּשָׁנוּ בְּמִצְוֹתָיו, וְצִוָּנוּ עַל מִצְוַת עֵרוּב.

בַּהֲדֵין עֵרוּבָא יְהֵא שָׁרֵא לָנָא לַאֲפוּיֵי וּלְבַשּׁוּלֵי וּלְאַצְלוּיֵי וּלְאַטְמוּנֵי וּלְאַדְלוּקֵי שְׁרָגָא וּלְתַקָּנָא וּלְמֶעְבַּד כָּל צָרְכָנָא, מִיּוֹמָא טָבָא לְשַׁבַּתָּא [לָנוּ וּלְכָל יִשְׂרָאֵל הַדָּרִים בָּעִיר הַזֹּאת].

כרפס	ורחץ	קדש
רחצה	מגיד	יחץ
כורך	מרור	מוציא מצה
ברך	צפון	שלחן עורך

	נרצה	הלל	

✌ Searching for Chametz ☙

Blessed are You, Hashem, our God, King of the Universe, Who has sanctified us with His commandments, and commanded us concerning the removal of chametz.

All chametz in my possession, which I have neither seen nor removed nor know about, shall be considered of no value and ownerless as the dust of the earth.

✌ Burning the Chametz ☙

All chametz products in my possession, which I have either seen or not, whether I have removed them or not, shall be considered of no value and ownerless, like the dust of the earth.

✌ Eruv Tavshilin ☙

Blessed are You, Hashem, our God, King of the Universe, Who has sanctified us with His commandments, and commanded us concerning the commandment of Eruv.

Through this Eruv, may we be permitted to bake, cook, fry, insulate, light a flame, prepare for and do whatever is necessary on the festival for the sake of the Sabbath (for ourselves and for the Jews who live in this city).

Kaddesh *Reciting the kiddush*	**Urechatz** *Washing hands*	**Karpas** *Dipping vegetables in salt water*
Yachatz *Breaking the middle matzoh*	**Maggid** *Recite the haggadah*	**Rachtzah** *Washing hands for the meal*
Motzi Matzoh *Blessings over the matzoh*	**Marror** *Bitter herbs*	**Korech** *Marror and matzoh sandwich*
Shulchan Orech *Serve the meal*	**Tzafun** *Partaking of the afikoman*	**Barech** *Grace after meals*
Hallel *Reciting the Hallel*	**Nirtzah** *Acceptance*	

❧ קַדֵּשׁ ❧

(כשחל יו"ט בשבת מתחילים כאן.)

וַיְהִי עֶרֶב וַיְהִי בֹקֶר

יוֹם הַשִּׁשִּׁי, וַיְכֻלּוּ הַשָּׁמַיִם וְהָאָרֶץ וְכָל-צְבָאָם: וַיְכַל אֱלֹהִים בַּיּוֹם הַשְּׁבִיעִי, מְלַאכְתּוֹ אֲשֶׁר עָשָׂה, וַיִּשְׁבֹּת בַּיּוֹם הַשְּׁבִיעִי, מִכָּל-מְלַאכְתּוֹ אֲשֶׁר עָשָׂה: וַיְבָרֶךְ אֱלֹהִים אֶת-יוֹם הַשְּׁבִיעִי, וַיְקַדֵּשׁ אֹתוֹ, כִּי בוֹ שָׁבַת מִכָּל-מְלַאכְתּוֹ, אֲשֶׁר-בָּרָא אֱלֹהִים לַעֲשׂוֹת:

סַבְרִי מָרָנָן וְרַבָּנָן וְרַבּוֹתַי:

בָּרוּךְ אַתָּה יְיָ, אֱלֹהֵינוּ מֶלֶךְ הָעוֹלָם, בּוֹרֵא פְּרִי הַגָּפֶן:

בָּרוּךְ אַתָּה יְיָ, אֱלֹהֵינוּ מֶלֶךְ הָעוֹלָם, אֲשֶׁר בָּחַר בָּנוּ מִכָּל-עָם, וְרוֹמְמָנוּ מִכָּל-לָשׁוֹן, וְקִדְּשָׁנוּ בְּמִצְוֹתָיו, וַתִּתֶּן-לָנוּ יְיָ אֱלֹהֵינוּ בְּאַהֲבָה (לשבת שַׁבָּתוֹת לִמְנוּחָה וּ)מוֹעֲדִים לְשִׂמְחָה, חַגִּים וּזְמַנִּים לְשָׂשׂוֹן אֶת-יוֹם (לשבת הַשַּׁבָּת הַזֶּה וְאֶת-יוֹם) חַג הַמַּצּוֹת הַזֶּה. זְמַן חֵרוּתֵנוּ, (לשבת בְּאַהֲבָה,) מִקְרָא קֹדֶשׁ, זֵכֶר לִיצִיאַת מִצְרָיִם. כִּי בָנוּ בָחַרְתָּ וְאוֹתָנוּ קִדַּשְׁתָּ מִכָּל-הָעַמִּים. (לשבת וְשַׁבָּת) וּמוֹעֲדֵי קָדְשֶׁךָ (לשבת בְּאַהֲבָה וּבְרָצוֹן) בְּשִׂמְחָה וּבְשָׂשׂוֹן הִנְחַלְתָּנוּ: בָּרוּךְ אַתָּה יְיָ, מְקַדֵּשׁ (לשבת הַשַּׁבָּת וְ)יִשְׂרָאֵל וְהַזְּמַנִּים:

(כשחל יו"ט במוצאי שבת מוסיפים כאן ברכות הבדלה.)

בָּרוּךְ אַתָּה יְיָ, אֱלֹהֵינוּ מֶלֶךְ הָעוֹלָם, בּוֹרֵא מְאוֹרֵי הָאֵשׁ:

בָּרוּךְ אַתָּה יְיָ, אֱלֹהֵינוּ מֶלֶךְ הָעוֹלָם, הַמַּבְדִּיל בֵּין קֹדֶשׁ לְחֹל בֵּין אוֹר לְחֹשֶׁךְ, בֵּין יִשְׂרָאֵל לָעַמִּים, בֵּין יוֹם הַשְּׁבִיעִי לְשֵׁשֶׁת יְמֵי הַמַּעֲשֶׂה. בֵּין קְדֻשַּׁת שַׁבָּת לִקְדֻשַּׁת יוֹם טוֹב הִבְדַּלְתָּ. וְאֶת-יוֹם הַשְּׁבִיעִי מִשֵּׁשֶׁת יְמֵי הַמַּעֲשֶׂה קִדַּשְׁתָּ. הִבְדַּלְתָּ וְקִדַּשְׁתָּ אֶת-עַמְּךָ יִשְׂרָאֵל בִּקְדֻשָּׁתֶךָ. בָּרוּךְ אַתָּה יְיָ, הַמַּבְדִּיל בֵּין קֹדֶשׁ לְקֹדֶשׁ:

בָּרוּךְ אַתָּה יְיָ, אֱלֹהֵינוּ מֶלֶךְ הָעוֹלָם, שֶׁהֶחֱיָנוּ וְקִיְּמָנוּ וְהִגִּיעָנוּ לַזְּמַן הַזֶּה:

৪১ Kaddesh ৪৬
Reciting the kiddush

On Friday night add:

There was evening and there was morning.

On the sixth day, the heavens and the earth and all their hosts were completed. And God completed, on the seventh day, His work which He had made, and He ceased on the seventh day, all His work in which He had been engaged. And God blessed the seventh day and sanctified it; because on it He ceased all His work which God had created to make.

Blessed are You, Hashem our God, King of the universe, Who creates the fruit of the vine.

Blessed are You, Hashem our God, King of the universe, Who has chosen and exalted us above all nations and has sanctified us with His commandments. And You, Hashem our God, has lovingly bestowed upon us (**Sabbath:** for rest), appointed times for happiness, holidays and seasons for joy, (**Sabbath:** this Sabbath day, and) this Feast of Matzos, season of our freedom, a holy convocation in remembrance of the Exodus from Egypt. You did choose and sanctify us above all peoples (**Sabbath:** and the Sabbath) and Your holy festivals (**Sabbath:** in love and favor) in happiness and joy You did grant us a heritage. Blessed are You, Hashem, Who sanctifies (**Sabbath:** the Sabbath,) Yisrael, and the appointed times.

On Saturday night add the following two paragraphs

Blessed are You, Hashem our God, King of the universe, Who creates the light of the fire.

Blessed are You, Hashem our God, King of the universe, Who has distinguished between the sacred and the secular, between light and darkness, between Yisrael and the nations, between the seventh day and the six working days. You have distinguished between the holiness of the Sabbath and the holiness of the Festival, and have sanctified the seventh day above the six working days. You have distinguished and sanctified Your people Yisrael with Your holiness. Blessed are You Hashem our God, Who distinguishes between holiness and holiness.

Blessed are You, Hashem our God, King of the universe, Who has granted us life and sustained us and permitted us to reach this season.

וּרְחַץ ∞

קודם אכילת הכרפס מביאים מים ונוטלים ידים בלי ברכה

כַּרְפַּס ∞

מטבילים כרפס במי-מלח ומברכים

בָּרוּךְ אַתָּה יְיָ, אֱלֹהֵינוּ מֶלֶךְ הָעוֹלָם, בּוֹרֵא פְּרִי הָאֲדָמָה:

יַחַץ ∞

עורך הסדר פורס את המצה האמצעית שבקערה לשני חלקים

מַגִּיד ∞

מגביהים את המצה ומתחילים באמירת ההגדה

הָא לַחְמָא עַנְיָא דִּי אֲכָלוּ אַבְהָתָנָא בְּאַרְעָא דְמִצְרָיִם. כָּל דִּכְפִין יֵיתֵי וְיֵכֹל, כָּל דִּצְרִיךְ יֵיתֵי וְיִפְסַח. הָשַׁתָּא הָכָא, לְשָׁנָה הַבָּאָה בְּאַרְעָא דְיִשְׂרָאֵל. הָשַׁתָּא עַבְדֵי, לְשָׁנָה הַבָּאָה בְּנֵי חוֹרִין:

מַה נִּשְׁתַּנָּה הַלַּיְלָה הַזֶּה מִכָּל הַלֵּילוֹת?

שֶׁבְּכָל הַלֵּילוֹת אָנוּ אוֹכְלִין חָמֵץ וּמַצָּה. הַלַּיְלָה הַזֶּה כֻּלּוֹ מַצָּה:

שֶׁבְּכָל הַלֵּילוֹת אָנוּ אוֹכְלִין שְׁאָר יְרָקוֹת הַלַּיְלָה הַזֶּה מָרוֹר:

שֶׁבְּכָל הַלֵּילוֹת אֵין אָנוּ מַטְבִּילִין אֲפִילוּ פַּעַם אֶחָת. הַלַּיְלָה הַזֶּה שְׁתֵּי פְעָמִים:

שֶׁבְּכָל הַלֵּילוֹת אָנוּ אוֹכְלִין בֵּין יוֹשְׁבִין וּבֵין מְסֻבִּין. הַלַּיְלָה הַזֶּה כֻּלָּנוּ מְסֻבִּין:

עֲבָדִים הָיִינוּ לְפַרְעֹה בְּמִצְרָיִם. וַיּוֹצִיאֵנוּ יְיָ אֱלֹהֵינוּ מִשָּׁם, בְּיָד חֲזָקָה וּבִזְרוֹעַ נְטוּיָה, וְאִלּוּ לֹא הוֹצִיא הַקָּדוֹשׁ בָּרוּךְ הוּא אֶת-אֲבוֹתֵינוּ מִמִּצְרַיִם, הֲרֵי

&‿ Urechatz ‿&
Washing hands
(Without a brachah)

&‿ Karpas ‿&
Dipping vegetable in salt water

Blessed are You, Hashem our God, King of the universe, Who creates the fruit of the earth.

&‿ Yachatz ‿&
Breaking the middle matzoh

&‿ Maggid ‿&
Recite the Haggadah
Raising the matzos, the leader declares:

This is the bread of affliction which our fathers ate in the land of Egypt. Let all who are hungry come and eat. Let all who are needy come and celebrate the Pesach. At present we are here; next year may we be in Eretz Yisrael. At present we are slaves; next year may we be free men.

The second cup of wine is poured and the youngest present asks the four questions:

Why is this night different from all other nights?

1. On all other nights we eat chametz and matzoh. Tonight, only matzoh.
2. On all other nights we eat any kind of herbs. Tonight, bitter herbs.
3. On all other nights we do not dip even once. Tonight, (we dip) twice.
4. On all other nights we eat either sitting or reclining. Tonight, we all recline.

The following reply is recited in unison:

We were slaves to Pharaoh in Egypt, but Hashem our God took us out from there with a mighty hand and an outstretched arm. Had not the Holy One, Blessed is He taken our fathers out from Egypt, then we,

אָנוּ וּבָנֵינוּ וּבְנֵי בָנֵינוּ, מְשֻׁעְבָּדִים הָיִינוּ לְפַרְעֹה בְּמִצְרָיִם. וַאֲפִילוּ כֻּלָּנוּ חֲכָמִים, כֻּלָּנוּ נְבוֹנִים, כֻּלָּנוּ זְקֵנִים, כֻּלָּנוּ יוֹדְעִים אֶת־הַתּוֹרָה, מִצְוָה עָלֵינוּ לְסַפֵּר בִּיצִיאַת מִצְרָיִם. וְכָל הַמַּרְבֶּה לְסַפֵּר בִּיצִיאַת מִצְרַיִם, הֲרֵי זֶה מְשֻׁבָּח:

מַעֲשֶׂה בְּרַבִּי אֱלִיעֶזֶר, וְרַבִּי יְהוֹשֻׁעַ, וְרַבִּי אֶלְעָזָר בֶּן־עֲזַרְיָה, וְרַבִּי עֲקִיבָא, וְרַבִּי טַרְפוֹן, שֶׁהָיוּ מְסֻבִּין בִּבְנֵי־בְרַק, וְהָיוּ מְסַפְּרִים בִּיצִיאַת מִצְרַיִם, כָּל־אוֹתוֹ הַלַּיְלָה, עַד שֶׁבָּאוּ תַלְמִידֵיהֶם וְאָמְרוּ לָהֶם: רַבּוֹתֵינוּ, הִגִּיעַ זְמַן קְרִיאַת שְׁמַע, שֶׁל שַׁחֲרִית:

אָמַר רַבִּי אֶלְעָזָר בֶּן־עֲזַרְיָה. הֲרֵי אֲנִי כְּבֶן שִׁבְעִים שָׁנָה, וְלֹא זָכִיתִי, שֶׁתֵּאָמֵר יְצִיאַת מִצְרַיִם בַּלֵּילוֹת. עַד שֶׁדְּרָשָׁהּ בֶּן זוֹמָא. שֶׁנֶּאֱמַר: לְמַעַן תִּזְכֹּר, אֶת יוֹם צֵאתְךָ מֵאֶרֶץ מִצְרַיִם, כֹּל יְמֵי חַיֶּיךָ. יְמֵי חַיֶּיךָ הַיָּמִים. כֹּל יְמֵי חַיֶּיךָ הַלֵּילוֹת. וַחֲכָמִים אוֹמְרִים: יְמֵי חַיֶּיךָ הָעוֹלָם הַזֶּה. כֹּל יְמֵי חַיֶּיךָ לְהָבִיא לִימוֹת הַמָּשִׁיחַ:

בָּרוּךְ הַמָּקוֹם. בָּרוּךְ הוּא. בָּרוּךְ שֶׁנָּתַן תּוֹרָה לְעַמּוֹ יִשְׂרָאֵל. בָּרוּךְ הוּא כְּנֶגֶד אַרְבָּעָה בָנִים דִּבְּרָה תוֹרָה. אֶחָד חָכָם, וְאֶחָד רָשָׁע, וְאֶחָד תָּם, וְאֶחָד שֶׁאֵינוֹ יוֹדֵעַ לִשְׁאוֹל:

חָכָם מָה הוּא אוֹמֵר? מָה הָעֵדֹת וְהַחֻקִּים וְהַמִּשְׁפָּטִים, אֲשֶׁר צִוָּה יְיָ אֱלֹהֵינוּ אֶתְכֶם? וְאַף אַתָּה אֱמָר־לוֹ כְּהִלְכוֹת הַפֶּסַח: אֵין מַפְטִירִין אַחַר הַפֶּסַח אֲפִיקוֹמָן:

רָשָׁע מָה הוּא אוֹמֵר? מָה הָעֲבֹדָה הַזֹּאת לָכֶם? לָכֶם וְלֹא לוֹ. וּלְפִי שֶׁהוֹצִיא אֶת־עַצְמוֹ מִן הַכְּלָל, כָּפַר בָּעִקָּר. וְאַף אַתָּה הַקְהֵה אֶת־שִׁנָּיו, וֶאֱמָר־לוֹ: בַּעֲבוּר זֶה, עָשָׂה יְיָ לִי, בְּצֵאתִי מִמִּצְרָיִם, לִי וְלֹא־לוֹ. אִלּוּ הָיָה שָׁם, לֹא הָיָה נִגְאָל:

תָּם מָה הוּא אוֹמֵר? מַה זֹּאת? וְאָמַרְתָּ אֵלָיו: בְּחֹזֶק יָד הוֹצִיאָנוּ יְיָ מִמִּצְרַיִם מִבֵּית עֲבָדִים:

our children and grandchildren would still be enslaved to Pharaoh in Egypt. Even if we all were wise, and perceptive, experienced, and versed in Torah, it would still be our duty to tell about the Exodus from Egypt. The more one tells about the Exodus, the more praiseworthy it is.

It happened that Rabbi Eliezer, Rabbi Yehoshua, Rabbi Elazar ben Azaryah, Rabbi Akiva and Rabbi Tarfon were reclining (at the Seder table) in Bnei Brak. They spent that entire night discussing the Exodus until their students came and said to them: "Our Teachers, it is time for the recitation of the morning *Shema*."

Rabbi Elazar ben Azaryah said: "I am like a seventy-year-old man and I have not succeeded in understanding why the Exodus from Egypt should be mentioned at night, until Ben Zoma explained it by quoting: "In order that you may remember the day you left Egypt all the days of Your life." The phrase *the days of Your life* indicates only the *days*, the additional word "all" indicates that the *nights* are meant as well. The sages, however, declare that *"the days of your life"* means the present world and *"all"* includes the messianic era.

Blessed be the Omnipresent; blessed is He.

Blessed be God Who has given the Torah to His people Yisrael; blessed is He. The Torah speaks concerning four sons: a wise one, a wicked one, a simple one, and one who is not able to ask (a question).

The wise son — What does he say? "What is the meaning of the testimonies, statutes, and laws which Hashem our God has commanded you?" Therefore explain to him the laws of the *Pesach* offering: that no dessert may be eaten after the Pesach sacrifice.

The wicked son — What does he say? "What does this service mean to you?" By the words "to you" he implies that this service is only for you—not for himself. By excluding himself from the community, he denies God. So tell him bluntly: "This is done on account of what Hashem did for me when I came out of Egypt." *For me, but not for him*; had he been there, he would not have been redeemed.

The simple son — What does he say? "What is this all about?" Tell him, "With a strong hand Hashem brought us out of Egypt from the house of slavery."

וְשֶׁאֵינוֹ יוֹדֵעַ לִשְׁאוֹל, אַתְּ פְּתַח לוֹ. שֶׁנֶּאֱמַר: וְהִגַּדְתָּ לְבִנְךָ, בַּיּוֹם הַהוּא לֵאמֹר: בַּעֲבוּר זֶה עָשָׂה יְיָ לִי, בְּצֵאתִי מִמִּצְרָיִם:

יָכוֹל מֵרֹאשׁ חֹדֶשׁ, תַּלְמוּד לוֹמַר בַּיּוֹם הַהוּא. אִי בַּיּוֹם הַהוּא. יָכוֹל מִבְּעוֹד יוֹם. תַּלְמוּד לוֹמַר. בַּעֲבוּר זֶה. בַּעֲבוּר זֶה לֹא אָמַרְתִּי, אֶלָּא בְּשָׁעָה שֶׁיֵּשׁ מַצָּה וּמָרוֹר מֻנָּחִים לְפָנֶיךָ:

מִתְּחִלָּה עוֹבְדֵי עֲבוֹדָה זָרָה הָיוּ אֲבוֹתֵינוּ. וְעַכְשָׁו קֵרְבָנוּ הַמָּקוֹם לַעֲבוֹדָתוֹ. שֶׁנֶּאֱמַר: וַיֹּאמֶר יְהוֹשֻׁעַ אֶל־כָּל־הָעָם. כֹּה אָמַר יְיָ אֱלֹהֵי יִשְׂרָאֵל, בְּעֵבֶר הַנָּהָר יָשְׁבוּ אֲבוֹתֵיכֶם מֵעוֹלָם, תֶּרַח אֲבִי אַבְרָהָם וַאֲבִי נָחוֹר. וַיַּעַבְדוּ אֱלֹהִים אֲחֵרִים: וָאֶקַּח אֶת־אֲבִיכֶם אֶת־אַבְרָהָם מֵעֵבֶר הַנָּהָר, וָאוֹלֵךְ אוֹתוֹ בְּכָל־אֶרֶץ כְּנָעַן. וָאַרְבֶּה אֶת־זַרְעוֹ, וָאֶתֶּן לוֹ אֶת־יִצְחָק: וָאֶתֵּן לְיִצְחָק אֶת־יַעֲקֹב וְאֶת־עֵשָׂו. וָאֶתֵּן לְעֵשָׂו אֶת־הַר שֵׂעִיר, לָרֶשֶׁת אוֹתוֹ. וְיַעֲקֹב וּבָנָיו יָרְדוּ מִצְרָיִם:

בָּרוּךְ שׁוֹמֵר הַבְטָחָתוֹ לְיִשְׂרָאֵל. בָּרוּךְ הוּא. שֶׁהַקָּדוֹשׁ בָּרוּךְ הוּא חִשַּׁב אֶת־הַקֵּץ, לַעֲשׂוֹת כְּמָה שֶׁאָמַר לְאַבְרָהָם אָבִינוּ בִּבְרִית בֵּין הַבְּתָרִים, שֶׁנֶּאֱמַר: וַיֹּאמֶר לְאַבְרָם יָדֹעַ תֵּדַע, כִּי־גֵר יִהְיֶה זַרְעֲךָ, בְּאֶרֶץ לֹא לָהֶם, וַעֲבָדוּם וְעִנּוּ אֹתָם אַרְבַּע מֵאוֹת שָׁנָה: וְגַם אֶת־הַגּוֹי אֲשֶׁר יַעֲבֹדוּ דָּן אָנֹכִי. וְאַחֲרֵי כֵן יֵצְאוּ, בִּרְכֻשׁ גָּדוֹל:

מכסים את המצות ומגביהים את הכוס

וְהִיא שֶׁעָמְדָה לַאֲבוֹתֵינוּ וְלָנוּ. שֶׁלֹּא אֶחָד בִּלְבָד, עָמַד עָלֵינוּ לְכַלּוֹתֵנוּ. אֶלָּא שֶׁבְּכָל דּוֹר וָדוֹר, עוֹמְדִים עָלֵינוּ לְכַלּוֹתֵנוּ. וְהַקָּדוֹשׁ בָּרוּךְ הוּא מַצִּילֵנוּ מִיָּדָם:

צֵא וּלְמַד, מַה בִּקֵּשׁ לָבָן הָאֲרַמִּי לַעֲשׂוֹת לְיַעֲקֹב אָבִינוּ. שֶׁפַּרְעֹה לֹא גָזַר אֶלָּא עַל הַזְּכָרִים, וְלָבָן בִּקֵּשׁ לַעֲקֹר אֶת־הַכֹּל, שֶׁנֶּאֱמַר: אֲרַמִּי אֹבֵד אָבִי, וַיֵּרֶד מִצְרַיְמָה, וַיָּגָר שָׁם בִּמְתֵי מְעָט.וַיְהִי שָׁם לְגוֹי גָּדוֹל, עָצוּם וָרָב:

As for the son who is unable to ask, you must open up the subject to him, as it is stated: "You shall tell your son on that day: This is on account of what Hashem did for me when I came out of Egypt."

One might think that the obligation to discuss the Exodus begins on the first day of the month of Nissan, but the Torah says: "You shall tell your son *on that day*" [the first day of Pesach]. One might think that the phrase *on that day* means that the story of the Exodus should be recited only in the daytime; therefore, the Torah says: "*This* is on account of what Hashem did for me." The word *this* refers to the time when matzoh and marror are placed before you—(on Pesach night when you are obliged to eat them).

At first our forefathers were idol worshipers, but now the Omnipresent has brought us near to His service, as it is stated: "Yehoshua said to all the people: so says Hashem God of Yisrael— Your fathers have always lived beyond the Euphrates River, Terach the father of Avraham and Nachor; they worshiped other gods. I took your father Avraham from the other side of the river and led him through all the land of Canaan. I multiplied his offspring and gave him Yitzchak. To Yitzchak I gave Yaakov and Eisav; to Eisav I gave Mount Seir to inherit, however Yaakov and his children went down to Egypt."

Blessed is He Who keeps His promise to Yisrael; blessed is He. The Holy One, Blessed is He, predetermined the time for our final deliverance in order to fulfill what He had said to our father Avraham in the Covenant between the Parts, as it is stated: "He said to Avram, you should certainly know that your offspring will be strangers in a land that is not their own, and they will be enslaved and afflicted for four hundred years; however, I will punish the nation that enslaved them, and afterwards they shall leave with great wealth."

Cover the matzos and raise the wine cup and say:

It is this that has stood by our forefathers and us. For not only one (enemy) has risen against us to annihilate us, but in every generation they rise against us. But the Holy One, Blessed is He, saves us from their hand.

The wine cup is put down.

Go out and learn what Lavan the Aramean tried to do to our father Yaakov. While Pharaoh decreed only against the (newborn) males, Lavan tried to uproot everything, as it is stated: "An Aramaean sought to destroy my father. Then he went down to Egypt and sojourned there few in number and there he became a great, mighty, and numerous nation."

וַיֵּרֶד מִצְרַיְמָה, אָנוּס עַל פִּי הַדִּבּוּר. וַיָּגָר שָׁם. מְלַמֵּד שֶׁלֹּא יָרַד יַעֲקֹב אָבִינוּ לְהִשְׁתַּקֵּעַ בְּמִצְרַיִם, אֶלָּא לָגוּר שָׁם, שֶׁנֶּאֱמַר: וַיֹּאמְרוּ אֶל־פַּרְעֹה, לָגוּר בָּאָרֶץ בָּאנוּ, כִּי אֵין מִרְעֶה לַצֹּאן אֲשֶׁר לַעֲבָדֶיךָ, כִּי כָבֵד הָרָעָב בְּאֶרֶץ כְּנָעַן. וְעַתָּה, יֵשְׁבוּ־נָא עֲבָדֶיךָ בְּאֶרֶץ גֹּשֶׁן: בִּמְתֵי מְעָט. כְּמָה שֶׁנֶּאֱמַר: בְּשִׁבְעִים נֶפֶשׁ, יָרְדוּ אֲבֹתֶיךָ מִצְרַיְמָה. וְעַתָּה, שָׂמְךָ יְיָ אֱלֹהֶיךָ, כְּכוֹכְבֵי הַשָּׁמַיִם לָרֹב.   וַיְהִי שָׁם לְגוֹי. מְלַמֵּד שֶׁהָיוּ יִשְׂרָאֵל מְצֻיָּנִים שָׁם: גָּדוֹל עָצוּם, כְּמָה שֶׁנֶּאֱמַר: וּבְנֵי יִשְׂרָאֵל, פָּרוּ וַיִּשְׁרְצוּ, וַיִּרְבּוּ וַיַּעַצְמוּ, בִּמְאֹד מְאֹד, וַתִּמָּלֵא הָאָרֶץ אֹתָם.   וָרָב. כְּמָה שֶׁנֶּאֱמַר: רְבָבָה כְּצֶמַח הַשָּׂדֶה נְתַתִּיךְ, וַתִּרְבִּי, וַתִּגְדְּלִי, וַתָּבֹאִי בַּעֲדִי עֲדָיִים: שָׁדַיִם נָכֹנוּ, וּשְׂעָרֵךְ צִמֵּחַ, וְאַתְּ עֵרֹם וְעֶרְיָה: וָאֶעֱבֹר עָלַיִךְ וָאֶרְאֵךְ מִתְבּוֹסֶסֶת בְּדָמָיִךְ וָאֹמַר לָךְ בְּדָמַיִךְ חֲיִי   וָאֹמַר לָךְ בְּדָמַיִךְ חֲיִי.

וַיָּרֵעוּ אֹתָנוּ הַמִּצְרִים וַיְעַנּוּנוּ. וַיִּתְּנוּ עָלֵינוּ עֲבֹדָה קָשָׁה: וַיָּרֵעוּ אֹתָנוּ הַמִּצְרִים. כְּמָה שֶׁנֶּאֱמַר: הָבָה נִתְחַכְּמָה לוֹ. פֶּן־יִרְבֶּה, וְהָיָה כִּי־תִקְרֶאנָה מִלְחָמָה, וְנוֹסַף גַּם הוּא עַל־שֹׂנְאֵינוּ, וְנִלְחַם־בָּנוּ וְעָלָה מִן־הָאָרֶץ:

וַיְעַנּוּנוּ. כְּמָה שֶׁנֶּאֱמַר: וַיָּשִׂימוּ עָלָיו שָׂרֵי מִסִּים, לְמַעַן עַנֹּתוֹ בְּסִבְלֹתָם: וַיִּבֶן עָרֵי מִסְכְּנוֹת לְפַרְעֹה, אֶת־פִּתֹם וְאֶת־רַעַמְסֵס: וַיִּתְּנוּ עָלֵינוּ עֲבֹדָה קָשָׁה. כְּמָה שֶׁנֶּאֱמַר: וַיַּעֲבִדוּ מִצְרַיִם אֶת־בְּנֵי יִשְׂרָאֵל בְּפָרֶךְ:

וַנִּצְעַק אֶל־יְיָ אֱלֹהֵי אֲבֹתֵינוּ, וַיִּשְׁמַע יְיָ אֶת־קֹלֵנוּ, וַיַּרְא אֶת־עָנְיֵנוּ, וְאֶת־עֲמָלֵנוּ, וְאֶת לַחֲצֵנוּ: וַנִּצְעַק אֶל־יְיָ אֱלֹהֵי אֲבֹתֵינוּ, כְּמָה שֶׁנֶּאֱמַר: וַיְהִי בַיָּמִים הָרַבִּים הָהֵם, וַיָּמָת מֶלֶךְ מִצְרַיִם, וַיֵּאָנְחוּ בְנֵי־יִשְׂרָאֵל מִן־הָעֲבֹדָה וַיִּזְעָקוּ. וַתַּעַל שַׁוְעָתָם אֶל־הָאֱלֹהִים מִן־הָעֲבֹדָה: וַיִּשְׁמַע יְיָ אֶת־קֹלֵנוּ. כְּמָה שֶׁנֶּאֱמַר: וַיִּשְׁמַע אֱלֹהִים אֶת־נַאֲקָתָם, וַיִּזְכֹּר אֱלֹהִים אֶת־בְּרִיתוֹ, אֶת־אַבְרָהָם, אֶת־יִצְחָק, וְאֶת יַעֲקֹב: וַיַּרְא אֶת־עָנְיֵנוּ: זוֹ פְּרִישׁוּת דֶּרֶךְ אֶרֶץ. כְּמָה שֶׁנֶּאֱמַר: וַיַּרְא אֱלֹהִים אֶת־בְּנֵי יִשְׂרָאֵל: וַיֵּדַע אֱלֹהִים: וְאֶת־עֲמָלֵנוּ: אֵלּוּ הַבָּנִים. כְּמָה שֶׁנֶּאֱמַר: כָּל־הַבֵּן הַיִּלּוֹד הַיְאֹרָה תַּשְׁלִיכֻהוּ, וְכָל־הַבַּת תְּחַיּוּן: וְאֶת לַחֲצֵנוּ: זֶה הַדְּחַק. כְּמָה שֶׁנֶּאֱמַר: וְגַם־רָאִיתִי אֶת־הַלַּחַץ, אֲשֶׁר מִצְרַיִם לֹחֲצִים אֹתָם:

He went down to Egypt, compelled by Divine decree. *He sojourned there* teaches that our father Yaakov did not come down to settle in Egypt but only to live there temporarily, as it says: "They (the sons of Yaakov) said to Pharaoh: 'We have come to sojourn in this land because there is no pasture for your servants' flocks, because the famine is severe in the land of Canaan. And now, please, let your servants dwell in the land of Goshen." *Few in number,* as it is stated: "With seventy souls your ancestors went down to Egypt, and now Hashem your God has made you as numerous as the stars in the sky." *There he became a nation* teaches that Yisrael were distinguished there. *Great, mighty,* as it says: "The children of Yisrael were fruitful and increased greatly; they multiplied and became very, very mighty, and the land was full of them." *And numerous,* as it says: "I made you as populous as the plants of the field; you grew up and wore choice adornments; your body developed and your hair grew long; yet, you were bare and naked. And I passed over you and saw you trampled in your blood and I said to you, 'Through your blood shall you live!' And I said to you, 'Through your blood shall you live!' "

"The Egyptians did evil to us and afflicted us and they imposed hard labor upon us." *The Egyptians did evil to us*, as it says:"Let us deal wisely with them lest they multiply, and, if we happen to be at war, they too may join our enemies and fight against us and then leave the country."

And afflicted us, as it says: "They set taskmasters over them in order to oppress them with their burdens; and they built Pisom and Raamses as storage-cities for Pharaoh." *They imposed hard labor upon us,* as it says: "The Egyptians imposed hard labor upon the children of Yisrael, with crushing harshness."

We cried out to Hashem, the God of our fathers and Hashem heard our cry and saw our affliction, our toil, and our oppression. *We cried to Hashem, the God of our fathers,* as it says: "It happened in the course of those many days that the king of Egypt died; the children of Yisrael sighed because of their labor and cried; their cry of servitude reached God." *Hashem heard our cry,* as it says: "God heard their groaning and God remembered His covenant with Avraham, with Yitzchak, and with Yaakov." *And saw our affliction,* that is, the withdrawal from family life, as it says:"God saw the children of Yisrael and God knew." *Our toil* refers to the children, as it says: "Every son that will be born you shall cast him into the River, but you shall let every daughter live." *Our oppression* refers to the pressure used upon them, as it says: "I have also seen how the Egyptians are oppressing them."

וַיּוֹצִאֵנוּ יְיָ מִמִּצְרַיִם, בְּיָד חֲזָקָה, וּבִזְרֹעַ נְטוּיָה, וּבְמֹרָא גָדוֹל וּבְאֹתוֹת וּבְמֹפְתִים:

וַיּוֹצִאֵנוּ יְיָ מִמִּצְרַיִם. לֹא עַל־יְדֵי מַלְאָךְ, וְלֹא עַל־יְדֵי שָׂרָף. וְלֹא עַל־יְדֵי שָׁלִיחַ. אֶלָּא הַקָּדוֹשׁ בָּרוּךְ הוּא בִּכְבוֹדוֹ וּבְעַצְמוֹ. שֶׁנֶּאֱמַר: וְעָבַרְתִּי בְאֶרֶץ מִצְרַיִם בַּלַּיְלָה הַזֶּה, וְהִכֵּיתִי כָל־בְּכוֹר בְּאֶרֶץ מִצְרַיִם, מֵאָדָם וְעַד בְּהֵמָה, וּבְכָל־אֱלֹהֵי מִצְרַיִם אֶעֱשֶׂה שְׁפָטִים אֲנִי יְיָ:

וְעָבַרְתִּי בְאֶרֶץ־מִצְרַיִם בַּלַּיְלָה הַזֶּה, אֲנִי וְלֹא מַלְאָךְ. וְהִכֵּיתִי כָל בְּכוֹר בְּאֶרֶץ־מִצְרַיִם. אֲנִי וְלֹא שָׂרָף. וּבְכָל־אֱלֹהֵי מִצְרַיִם אֶעֱשֶׂה שְׁפָטִים, אֲנִי וְלֹא הַשָּׁלִיחַ. אֲנִי יְיָ. אֲנִי הוּא וְלֹא אַחֵר:

בְּיָד חֲזָקָה. זוֹ הַדֶּבֶר. כְּמָה שֶׁנֶּאֱמַר: הִנֵּה יַד־יְיָ הוֹיָה, בְּמִקְנְךָ אֲשֶׁר בַּשָּׂדֶה, בַּסּוּסִים בַּחֲמֹרִים בַּגְּמַלִּים, בַּבָּקָר וּבַצֹּאן, דֶּבֶר כָּבֵד מְאֹד: וּבִזְרֹעַ נְטוּיָה. זוֹ הַחֶרֶב. כְּמָה שֶׁנֶּאֱמַר: וְחַרְבּוֹ שְׁלוּפָה בְּיָדוֹ, נְטוּיָה עַל־יְרוּשָׁלָיִם: וּבְמֹרָא גָדוֹל, זוֹ גִלּוּי שְׁכִינָה. כְּמָה שֶׁנֶּאֱמַר: אוֹ הֲנִסָּה אֱלֹהִים, לָבוֹא לָקַחַת לוֹ גוֹי מִקֶּרֶב גּוֹי, בְּמַסֹּת בְּאֹתֹת וּבְמוֹפְתִים וּבְמִלְחָמָה, וּבְיָד חֲזָקָה וּבִזְרֹעַ נְטוּיָה, וּבְמוֹרָאִים גְּדֹלִים. כְּכֹל אֲשֶׁר־עָשָׂה לָכֶם יְיָ אֱלֹהֵיכֶם בְּמִצְרַיִם, לְעֵינֶיךָ: וּבְאֹתוֹת. זֶה הַמַּטֶּה, כְּמָה שֶׁנֶּאֱמַר: וְאֶת־הַמַּטֶּה הַזֶּה תִּקַּח בְּיָדֶךָ. אֲשֶׁר תַּעֲשֶׂה־בּוֹ אֶת־הָאֹתֹת: וּבְמֹפְתִים. זֶה הַדָּם. כְּמָה שֶׁנֶּאֱמַר: וְנָתַתִּי מוֹפְתִים, בַּשָּׁמַיִם וּבָאָרֶץ

נוֹהֲגִים לְהַטִּיף מְעַט מִן הַכּוֹס בְּעֵת אֲמִירַת דָּם וָאֵשׁ, וְגַם בַּאֲמִירַת דַּם צְפַרְדֵּעַ, וְכוּ׳, וְגַם בַּאֲמִירַת דְּצַ״ךְ עֲדַ״שׁ וְכוּ׳

דָּם. וָאֵשׁ. וְתִמְרוֹת עָשָׁן:

"Hashem brought us out of Egypt with a mighty hand and with an outstretched arm, with great awe, with signs and wonders."

Hashem brought us out of Egypt not by an angel, not by a seraph, not by a messenger, but the Holy One, blessed is He, in His glory, Himself, as it says: "I will pass through the land of Egypt on that night; I will smite all the firstborn in the land of Egypt from man unto beast; on all the gods of Egypt I will execute judgments; I am Hashem."

I will pass through the land of Egypt on that night, I and not an angel; *I will smite all the firstborn in the land of Egypt,* I and not a seraph; *on all the gods of Egypt I will execute judgments,* I and not a messenger; *I am Hashem,* it is I and none other.

With a Mighty hand refers to the cattle disease (pestilence), as it says: "Behold the *hand* of Hashem will strike your cattle which are in the field, the horses, the donkeys, the camels, the herds, and the flocks—a very severe pestilence." *With an outstretched arm* means the sword, as it says: "His drawn sword in his hand, *outstretched* over Jerusalem." *With great awe* alludes to the Divine revelation, as it says: "Has God ever attempted to take unto Himself, a nation from the midst of another nation by trials, miraculous signs and wonders, by war and with a mighty hand and outstretched arm and by awesome revelations, just Hashem your God did everything for you in Egypt, before your eyes?" *With signs* refers to the miracles performed with the staff (of Moses), as it says: "Take this staff in your hand, that you may perform the miraculous signs with it." *With wonders* alludes to the plague of blood, as it says: "I will show wonders in the sky and on the earth."

As one spills three drops of wine, he declares:

"Blood, fire, and columns of smoke."

דָּבָר אַחֵר. בְּיָד חֲזָקָה שְׁתַּיִם. וּבִזְרֹעַ נְטוּיָה שְׁתַּיִם. וּבְמֹרָא גָּדוֹל שְׁתַּיִם. וּבְאֹתוֹת שְׁתַּיִם. וּבְמֹפְתִים שְׁתַּיִם: אֵלּוּ עֶשֶׂר מַכּוֹת שֶׁהֵבִיא הַקָּדוֹשׁ בָּרוּךְ הוּא עַל־הַמִּצְרִים בְּמִצְרַיִם, וְאֵלּוּ הֵן:

דָּם. צְפַרְדֵּעַ. כִּנִּים. עָרוֹב. דֶּבֶר. שְׁחִין. בָּרָד. אַרְבֶּה. חֹשֶׁךְ. מַכַּת בְּכוֹרוֹת:

רַבִּי יְהוּדָה הָיָה נוֹתֵן בָּהֶם סִמָּנִים:

דְּצַ"ךְ עַדַ"שׁ בְּאַחַ"ב:

רַבִּי יוֹסֵי הַגְּלִילִי אוֹמֵר: מִנַּיִן אַתָּה אוֹמֵר, שֶׁלָּקוּ הַמִּצְרִים בְּמִצְרַיִם עֶשֶׂר מַכּוֹת, וְעַל הַיָּם, לָקוּ חֲמִשִּׁים מַכּוֹת? בְּמִצְרַיִם מָה הוּא אוֹמֵר? וַיֹּאמְרוּ הַחַרְטֻמִּם אֶל־פַּרְעֹה, אֶצְבַּע אֱלֹהִים הוּא. וְעַל הַיָּם מָה הוּא אוֹמֵר? וַיַּרְא יִשְׂרָאֵל אֶת־הַיָּד הַגְּדֹלָה, אֲשֶׁר עָשָׂה יְיָ בְּמִצְרַיִם, וַיִּירְאוּ הָעָם אֶת־יְיָ. וַיַּאֲמִינוּ בַּיָי, וּבְמֹשֶׁה עַבְדּוֹ. כַּמָּה לָקוּ בְאֶצְבַּע, עֶשֶׂר מַכּוֹת: אֱמוֹר מֵעַתָּה, בְּמִצְרַיִם לָקוּ עֶשֶׂר מַכּוֹת, וְעַל־הַיָּם, לָקוּ חֲמִשִּׁים מַכּוֹת:

רַבִּי אֱלִיעֶזֶר אוֹמֵר: מִנַּיִן שֶׁכָּל־מַכָּה וּמַכָּה, שֶׁהֵבִיא הַקָּדוֹשׁ בָּרוּךְ הוּא עַל הַמִּצְרִים בְּמִצְרַיִם, הָיְתָה שֶׁל אַרְבַּע מַכּוֹת? שֶׁנֶּאֱמַר: יְשַׁלַּח־בָּם חֲרוֹן אַפּוֹ, עֶבְרָה וָזַעַם וְצָרָה. מִשְׁלַחַת מַלְאֲכֵי רָעִים. עֶבְרָה אַחַת. וָזַעַם שְׁתַּיִם. וְצָרָה שָׁלֹשׁ. מִשְׁלַחַת מַלְאֲכֵי רָעִים אַרְבַּע: אֱמוֹר מֵעַתָּה, בְּמִצְרַיִם לָקוּ אַרְבָּעִים מַכּוֹת, וְעַל הַיָּם לָקוּ מָאתַיִם מַכּוֹת:

רַבִּי עֲקִיבָא אוֹמֵר: מִנַּיִן שֶׁכָּל־מַכָּה וּמַכָּה, שֶׁהֵבִיא הַקָּדוֹשׁ בָּרוּךְ הוּא עַל הַמִּצְרִים בְּמִצְרַיִם, הָיְתָה שֶׁל חָמֵשׁ מַכּוֹת? שֶׁנֶּאֱמַר: יְשַׁלַּח־בָּם חֲרוֹן אַפּוֹ, עֶבְרָה וָזַעַם וְצָרָה. מִשְׁלַחַת מַלְאֲכֵי רָעִים. חֲרוֹן אַפּוֹ אַחַת. עֶבְרָה שְׁתַּיִם. וָזַעַם שָׁלֹשׁ. וְצָרָה אַרְבַּע. מִשְׁלַחַת מַלְאֲכֵי רָעִים חָמֵשׁ: אֱמוֹר מֵעַתָּה, בְּמִצְרַיִם לָקוּ חֲמִשִּׁים מַכּוֹת, וְעַל הַיָּם לָקוּ חֲמִשִּׁים וּמָאתַיִם מַכּוֹת:

Another explanation of the preceding verse: [Each two-word phrase represents two plagues, hence] *mighty hand*, two; *outstretched arm*, two; *great awe*; two; *signs*, two; *wonders*, two. These are the Ten Plagues which the Holy One, Blessed is He, brought upon the Egyptians in Egypt, namely:

**1. Blood   2. Frogs   3. Lice   4. Wild Animals
5. Pestilence   6. Boils   7. Hail   8. Locusts
9. Darkness   10. Death of the Firstborn**

Rabbi Yehudah abbreviated the Ten Plagues by composing
three words from their Hebrew initials:

D'tzach, Adash, B'achab

Rabbi Yose the Galilean says: How does one derive that the Egyptians suffered ten plagues in Egypt but suffered fifty plagues at the Sea? Concerning the plagues in Egypt the Torah states that "the magicians said to Pharaoh, "It is the *finger* of God." However, at the Sea, the Torah relates that "Yisrael saw the great *hand* which Hashem laid upon the Egyptians, and the people revered Hashem and they believed in Hashem and in Moshe His servant." It reasons that if they suffered ten plagues in Egypt, (where they were struck with a 'finger') they must have been made to suffer fifty plagues at the Sea (where they were struck with a 'hand').

Rabbi Eliezer says: How does one derive that every plague that the Holy One, Blessed is He inflicted upon the Egyptians in Egypt was equal (in intensity) to four plagues? As it says: "He sent upon them His fierce anger, wrath, fury and trouble, a band of evil messengers." [Since each plague was comprised of] 1) wrath, 2) fury, 3) trouble and 4) a band of evil messengers, therefore conclude that they must have suffered forty plagues in Egypt and two hundred at the Sea.

Rabbi Akiva says: How does one derive that every plague that the Holy One, Blessed is He inflicted upon the Egyptians in Egypt was equal (in intensity) to five plagues? As it says: "He sent upon them His fierce anger, wrath, fury and trouble, a band of evil messengers." [Since each plague was comprised of] 1)fierce anger 2)wrath 3)fury 4)trouble and 5) a band of evil messengers, therefore conclude that they must have suffered fifty plagues in Egypt and two hundred and fifty at the Sea.

כַּמָּה מַעֲלוֹת טוֹבוֹת לַמָּקוֹם עָלֵינוּ:

דַּיֵּנוּ:   אִלּוּ הוֹצִיאָנוּ מִמִּצְרַיִם, וְלֹא עָשָׂה בָהֶם שְׁפָטִים,

דַּיֵּנוּ:   אִלּוּ עָשָׂה בָהֶם שְׁפָטִים, וְלֹא עָשָׂה בֵאלֹהֵיהֶם,

דַּיֵּנוּ:   אִלּוּ עָשָׂה בֵאלֹהֵיהֶם, וְלֹא הָרַג אֶת־בְּכוֹרֵיהֶם,

דַּיֵּנוּ:   אִלּוּ הָרַג אֶת־בְּכוֹרֵיהֶם, וְלֹא נָתַן לָנוּ אֶת־מָמוֹנָם,

דַּיֵּנוּ:   אִלּוּ נָתַן לָנוּ אֶת־מָמוֹנָם, וְלֹא קָרַע לָנוּ אֶת־הַיָּם,

דַּיֵּנוּ:   אִלּוּ קָרַע לָנוּ אֶת־הַיָּם, וְלֹא הֶעֱבִירָנוּ בְתוֹכוֹ בֶּחָרָבָה

דַּיֵּנוּ:   אִלּוּ הֶעֱבִירָנוּ בְתוֹכוֹ בֶּחָרָבָה, וְלֹא שִׁקַּע צָרֵינוּ בְּתוֹכוֹ,

דַּיֵּנוּ:   אִלּוּ שִׁקַּע צָרֵינוּ בְּתוֹכוֹ, וְלֹא סִפֵּק צָרְכֵּנוּ בַּמִּדְבָּר אַרְבָּעִים שָׁנָה,

דַּיֵּנוּ:   אִלּוּ סִפֵּק צָרְכֵּנוּ בַּמִּדְבָּר אַרְבָּעִים שָׁנָה, וְלֹא הֶאֱכִילָנוּ אֶת־הַמָּן,

דַּיֵּנוּ:   אִלּוּ הֶאֱכִילָנוּ אֶת־הַמָּן, וְלֹא נָתַן לָנוּ אֶת־הַשַּׁבָּת,

דַּיֵּנוּ:   אִלּוּ נָתַן לָנוּ אֶת־הַשַּׁבָּת, וְלֹא קֵרְבָנוּ לִפְנֵי הַר סִינַי,

דַּיֵּנוּ:   אִלּוּ קֵרְבָנוּ לִפְנֵי הַר סִינַי, וְלֹא נָתַן לָנוּ אֶת־הַתּוֹרָה,

דַּיֵּנוּ:   אִלּוּ נָתַן לָנוּ אֶת־הַתּוֹרָה, וְלֹא הִכְנִיסָנוּ לְאֶרֶץ יִשְׂרָאֵל,

דַּיֵּנוּ:   אִלּוּ הִכְנִיסָנוּ לְאֶרֶץ יִשְׂרָאֵל, וְלֹא בָנָה לָנוּ אֶת־בֵּית הַבְּחִירָה,

עַל אַחַת כַּמָּה וְכַמָּה טוֹבָה כְפוּלָה וּמְכֻפֶּלֶת לַמָּקוֹם עָלֵינוּ: שֶׁהוֹצִיאָנוּ מִמִּצְרַיִם, וְעָשָׂה בָהֶם שְׁפָטִים, וְעָשָׂה בֵאלֹהֵיהֶם, וְהָרַג אֶת־בְּכוֹרֵיהֶם, וְנָתַן לָנוּ אֶת־מָמוֹנָם, וְקָרַע לָנוּ אֶת־הַיָּם, וְהֶעֱבִירָנוּ בְתוֹכוֹ בֶּחָרָבָה, וְשִׁקַּע צָרֵינוּ בְּתוֹכוֹ, וְסִפֵּק צָרְכֵּנוּ בַּמִּדְבָּר אַרְבָּעִים שָׁנָה, וְהֶאֱכִילָנוּ אֶת־הַמָּן, וְנָתַן לָנוּ אֶת־הַשַּׁבָּת, וְקֵרְבָנוּ לִפְנֵי הַר סִינַי, וְנָתַן לָנוּ אֶת־הַתּוֹרָה, וְהִכְנִיסָנוּ לְאֶרֶץ יִשְׂרָאֵל, וּבָנָה לָנוּ אֶת־בֵּית הַבְּחִירָה, לְכַפֵּר עַל־כָּל־עֲוֹנוֹתֵינוּ.

God has bestowed many favors upon us.

Had He brought us out of Egypt, and not executed judgments against them (the Egyptians), it would have been enough—*Da'yeinu*

Had He executed judgments against them (the Egyptians), and not against their gods, it would have been enough—*Da'yeinu*

Had He executed judgments against their gods and not put to death their firstborn, it would have been enough—*Da'yeinu*

Had He put to death their firstborn, and not given us their riches, it would have been enough—*Da'yeinu*

Had He given us their riches, and not split the Sea for us, it would have been enough—*Da'yeinu*

Had He split the Sea for us, and not led us through it on dry land, it would have been enough—*Da'yeinu*

Had He led us through it on dry land, and not drowned our oppressors in it, it would have been enough—*Da'yeinu*

Had He drowned our oppressors in it, and not provided for our needs in the desert for forty years, it would have been enough—*Da'yeinu*

Had He provided for our needs in the desert for forty years, and not fed us the manna, it would have been enough—*Da'yeinu*

Had He fed us the manna, and not given us the Sabbath, it would have been enough—*Da'yeinu*

Had He given us the Sabbath, and not brought us before Mount Sinai, it would have been enough—*Da'yeinu*

Had He brought us before Mount Sinai, and not given us the Torah, it would have been enough—*Da'yeinu*

Had He given us the Torah, and not brought us into Eretz Yisrael, it would have been enough—*Da'yeinu*

Had He brought us into Eretz Yisrael, and not built the *Bais Hamikdash* for us, it would have been enough —*Da'yeinu*

Thus, how much more so, then should we be grateful to the Omnipresent for the numerous favors that He bestowed upon us: He brought us out of Egypt, and executed judgments against the Egyptians and against their gods; and slew their firstborn; He gave us their wealth and split the Sea for us; He led us through it on dry land, and drowned our oppressors in it; He provided our needs in the desert for forty years, and fed us the manna; He gave us the Sabbath, and brought us before Mount Sinai; He gave us the Torah, and brought us to Eretz Yisrael; He built the *Bais Hamikdash* for us, to atone for all our sins.

רַבָּן גַּמְלִיאֵל הָיָה אוֹמֵר: כָּל שֶׁלֹּא אָמַר שְׁלֹשָׁה דְבָרִים אֵלּוּ בַּפֶּסַח,
לֹא יָצָא יְדֵי חוֹבָתוֹ, וְאֵלּוּ הֵן:

פֶּסַח מַצָּה וּמָרוֹר:

פֶּסַח שֶׁהָיוּ אֲבוֹתֵינוּ אוֹכְלִים, בִּזְמַן שֶׁבֵּית הַמִּקְדָּשׁ הָיָה קַיָּם, עַל שׁוּם מָה?
עַל שׁוּם שֶׁפָּסַח הַקָּדוֹשׁ בָּרוּךְ הוּא, עַל בָּתֵּי אֲבוֹתֵינוּ בְּמִצְרַיִם, שֶׁנֶּאֱמַר:
וַאֲמַרְתֶּם זֶבַח פֶּסַח הוּא לַיי, אֲשֶׁר פָּסַח עַל בָּתֵּי בְנֵי יִשְׂרָאֵל בְּמִצְרַיִם, בְּנָגְפּוֹ
אֶת־מִצְרַיִם וְאֶת־בָּתֵּינוּ הִצִּיל, וַיִּקֹּד הָעָם וַיִּשְׁתַּחֲווּ.

יגביה המצה ויאמר

מַצָּה זוֹ שֶׁאָנוּ אוֹכְלִים, עַל שׁוּם מָה? עַל שׁוּם שֶׁלֹּא הִסְפִּיק בְּצֵקָם שֶׁל
אֲבוֹתֵינוּ לְהַחֲמִיץ, עַד שֶׁנִּגְלָה עֲלֵיהֶם מֶלֶךְ מַלְכֵי הַמְּלָכִים, הַקָּדוֹשׁ בָּרוּךְ הוּא,
וּגְאָלָם, שֶׁנֶּאֱמַר: וַיֹּאפוּ אֶת־הַבָּצֵק, אֲשֶׁר הוֹצִיאוּ מִמִּצְרַיִם, עֻגֹת מַצּוֹת, כִּי לֹא
חָמֵץ: כִּי גֹרְשׁוּ מִמִּצְרַיִם, וְלֹא יָכְלוּ לְהִתְמַהְמֵהַּ, וְגַם צֵדָה לֹא עָשׂוּ לָהֶם.

יגביה המרור ויאמר

מָרוֹר זֶה שֶׁאָנוּ אוֹכְלִים, עַל שׁוּם מָה? עַל שׁוּם שֶׁמֵּרְרוּ הַמִּצְרִים אֶת־חַיֵּי
אֲבוֹתֵינוּ בְּמִצְרַיִם, שֶׁנֶּאֱמַר: וַיְמָרְרוּ אֶת־חַיֵּיהֶם בַּעֲבֹדָה קָשָׁה, בְּחֹמֶר וּבִלְבֵנִים,
וּבְכָל־עֲבֹדָה בַּשָּׂדֶה: אֵת כָּל־עֲבֹדָתָם, אֲשֶׁר עָבְדוּ בָהֶם בְּפָרֶךְ.

בְּכָל־דּוֹר וָדוֹר חַיָּב אָדָם לִרְאוֹת אֶת־עַצְמוֹ, כְּאִלּוּ הוּא יָצָא מִמִּצְרַיִם,
שֶׁנֶּאֱמַר: וְהִגַּדְתָּ לְבִנְךָ בַּיּוֹם הַהוּא לֵאמֹר: בַּעֲבוּר זֶה עָשָׂה יְיָ לִי, בְּצֵאתִי
מִמִּצְרַיִם. לֹא אֶת־אֲבוֹתֵינוּ בִּלְבָד, גָּאַל הַקָּדוֹשׁ בָּרוּךְ הוּא, אֶלָּא אַף אוֹתָנוּ גָּאַל
עִמָּהֶם, שֶׁנֶּאֱמַר: וְאוֹתָנוּ הוֹצִיא מִשָּׁם, לְמַעַן הָבִיא אֹתָנוּ, לָתֶת לָנוּ אֶת־הָאָרֶץ
אֲשֶׁר נִשְׁבַּע לַאֲבֹתֵנוּ.

יגביה הכום, יכסה המצות ויאמר

לְפִיכָךְ אֲנַחְנוּ חַיָּבִים לְהוֹדוֹת, לְהַלֵּל, לְשַׁבֵּחַ, לְפָאֵר, לְרוֹמֵם, לְהַדֵּר,
לְבָרֵךְ, לְעַלֵּה, וּלְקַלֵּס, לְמִי שֶׁעָשָׂה לַאֲבוֹתֵינוּ וְלָנוּ אֶת־כָּל־הַנִּסִּים הָאֵלּוּ.

Rabban Gamliel used to say: Whoever has not explained these three things on Pesach has not fulfilled his duty, namely:

Pesach, the Pesach Offering;
Matzoh, the Unleavened Bread;
Marror, the Bitter Herbs.

Pesach — Why did our fathers eat the Pesach Offering during the period of the *Bais Hamikdash?* It is because the Holy One, Blessed is He, passed over the houses of our fathers in Egypt, as it says: "You shall say: It is the Pesach offering for Hashem, Who passed over the houses of Bnei Yisrael in Egypt when He smote the Egyptians and spared our houses. The people bowed and prostrated themselves."

One raises the Matzoh and says:Matzoh

Matzoh — Why do we eat this matzoh? It is because the dough of our fathers did not have time to ferment before the King of kings, the Holy one, Blessed is He revealed Himself to them and redeemed them, as it says: "They baked the dough which they had brought out of Egypt into unleavened cakes, because it did not ferment, for they were driven out of Egypt and could not delay, nor had they prepared any provisions for their journey."

One raises the Marror and says:

Maror — Why do we eat this bitter herb? It is because the Egyptians embittered the lives of our fathers in Egypt, as it says: "They embittered their lives with hard labor, with clay and bricks, and with all kinds of labor in the field; whatever labor they made them perform was with crushing harshness."

In every generation it is man's duty to regard himself as though he personally had come out of Egypt, as it says: "You shall tell your son on that day: This is on account of what Hashem did for *me* when I came out of Egypt." It was not only our fathers whom the Holy One redeemed from slavery; we, too, were redeemed with them, as it says: "He took us out from there so that He might take us and give us the land which He had sworn to our fathers."

The matzoh is covered and the cup of wine is raised until the conclusion of the blessing, 'Ga-al Yisrael', so that the Hallel is recited over wine:

Therefore it is our duty to thank, praise, pay tribute, glorify, exalt, honor, bless and acclaim the One Who performed all these miracles

הוֹצִיאָנוּ מֵעַבְדוּת לְחֵרוּת, מִיָּגוֹן לְשִׂמְחָה, וּמֵאֵבֶל לְיוֹם טוֹב, וּמֵאֲפֵלָה לְאוֹר גָּדוֹל, וּמִשִּׁעְבּוּד לִגְאֻלָּה. וְנֹאמַר לְפָנָיו שִׁירָה חֲדָשָׁה. הַלְלוּיָהּ:

מניחים את הכוס ומגלים את המצות

הַלְלוּיָהּ הַלְלוּ עַבְדֵי יְיָ. הַלְלוּ אֶת־שֵׁם יְיָ. יְהִי שֵׁם יְיָ מְבֹרָךְ מֵעַתָּה וְעַד עוֹלָם: מִמִּזְרַח־שֶׁמֶשׁ עַד מְבוֹאוֹ. מְהֻלָּל שֵׁם יְיָ. רָם עַל־כָּל־גּוֹיִם יְיָ. עַל הַשָּׁמַיִם כְּבוֹדוֹ: מִי כַּיְיָ אֱלֹהֵינוּ. הַמַּגְבִּיהִי לָשָׁבֶת: הַמַּשְׁפִּילִי לִרְאוֹת בַּשָּׁמַיִם וּבָאָרֶץ: מְקִימִי מֵעָפָר דָּל. מֵאַשְׁפֹּת יָרִים אֶבְיוֹן: לְהוֹשִׁיבִי עִם־נְדִיבִים. עִם נְדִיבֵי עַמּוֹ: מוֹשִׁיבִי עֲקֶרֶת הַבַּיִת אֵם הַבָּנִים שְׂמֵחָה. הַלְלוּיָהּ:

בְּצֵאת יִשְׂרָאֵל מִמִּצְרָיִם, בֵּית יַעֲקֹב מֵעַם לֹעֵז: הָיְתָה יְהוּדָה לְקָדְשׁוֹ. יִשְׂרָאֵל מַמְשְׁלוֹתָיו: הַיָּם רָאָה וַיָּנֹס, הַיַּרְדֵּן יִסֹּב לְאָחוֹר: הֶהָרִים רָקְדוּ כְאֵילִים. גְּבָעוֹת כִּבְנֵי־צֹאן: מַה־לְּךָ הַיָּם כִּי תָנוּס. הַיַּרְדֵּן תִּסֹּב לְאָחוֹר: הֶהָרִים תִּרְקְדוּ כְאֵילִים. גְּבָעוֹת כִּבְנֵי־צֹאן: מִלִּפְנֵי אָדוֹן חוּלִי אָרֶץ. מִלִּפְנֵי אֱלוֹהַ יַעֲקֹב: הַהֹפְכִי הַצּוּר אֲגַם־מָיִם. חַלָּמִישׁ לְמַעְיְנוֹ־מָיִם.

כל אחד יקח כוסו בידו

בָּרוּךְ אַתָּה יְיָ, אֱלֹהֵינוּ מֶלֶךְ הָעוֹלָם, אֲשֶׁר גְּאָלָנוּ וְגָאַל אֶת־אֲבוֹתֵינוּ מִמִּצְרַיִם, וְהִגִּיעָנוּ הַלַּיְלָה הַזֶּה, לֶאֱכָל־בּוֹ מַצָּה וּמָרוֹר. כֵּן, יְיָ אֱלֹהֵינוּ וֵאלֹהֵי אֲבוֹתֵינוּ, יַגִּיעֵנוּ לְמוֹעֲדִים וְלִרְגָלִים אֲחֵרִים, הַבָּאִים לִקְרָאתֵנוּ לְשָׁלוֹם. שְׂמֵחִים בְּבִנְיַן עִירֶךָ, וְשָׂשִׂים בַּעֲבוֹדָתֶךָ, וְנֹאכַל שָׁם מִן הַזְּבָחִים וּמִן הַפְּסָחִים (במוצאי שבת אומרים מִן הַפְּסָחִים וּמִן הַזְּבָחִים), אֲשֶׁר יַגִּיעַ דָּמָם, עַל קִיר מִזְבַּחֲךָ לְרָצוֹן, וְנוֹדֶה לְךָ שִׁיר חָדָשׁ עַל גְּאֻלָּתֵנוּ, וְעַל פְּדוּת נַפְשֵׁנוּ:בָּרוּךְ אַתָּה יְיָ, גָּאַל יִשְׂרָאֵל:

כוס שני

בָּרוּךְ אַתָּה יְיָ, אֱלֹהֵינוּ מֶלֶךְ הָעוֹלָם, בּוֹרֵא פְּרִי הַגָּפֶן:

for our fathers and for us. He took us out from slavery to freedom, from grief to joy, from mourning to a festival, from darkness to a great light, from slavery to redemption. We will recite a new song before Him! Halleluyah!

Praise Hashem! Praise, you servants of Hashem, praise the Name of Hashem. Blessed be the Name of Hashem from now and forever. From the rising of the sun to its setting, Hashem's Name is to be praised. High above all nations is Hashem; above the heavens is His glory. Who is like Hashem our God, Who though enthroned on high, looks down upon heaven and earth? He raises the poor man out of the dust and lifts the needy one out of the trash heap, to seat them with nobles, with the nobles of His people. He turns the barren wife into a happy mother of children. Halleluyah!

When Yisrael went out of Egypt, Yaakov's household from a people of strange speech, Yehudah became His sanctuary, Yisrael His dominion. The Sea saw and fled; the Jordan turned backward. The mountains skipped like rams, and the hills like lambs. Why is it, Sea, that you flee? Why, Jordan, do you turn backward? Mountains, why do you skip like rams? Hills, why do you leap like lambs? Earth, tremble at Hashem's presence, at the presence of the God of Yaakov, Who turns the rock into a pond of water, the flint into a flowing fountain.

Blessed are You, Hashem our God, King of the universe, Who has redeemed us and our fathers from Egypt and enabled us to reach this night that we may eat matzoh and marror. So, Hashem our God and God of our fathers, enable us to reach also the forthcoming holidays and festivals in peace, rejoicing in the rebuilding of Your city, and joyful at Your service. There we shall eat of the offerings and Pesach sacrifices (**On Saturday night read:** of the Pesach sacrifices and offerings) whose blood will be acceptably placed upon Your altar. We shall sing a new song of praise to You for our redemption and for the liberation of our souls. Blessed are You, Hashem, Who has redeemed Yisrael.

Over the second cup of wine, one recites:

Blessed are You, Hashem our God, King of the universe, Who creates the fruit of the vine.

४ רָחְצָה ৪

נוטלים ידים ומברכים:

בָּרוּךְ אַתָּה יְיָ אֱלֹהֵינוּ מֶלֶךְ הָעוֹלָם, אֲשֶׁר קִדְּשָׁנוּ בְּמִצְוֹתָיו, וְצִוָּנוּ עַל נְטִילַת יָדָיִם:

४ מוֹצִיא מַצָּה ৪

נוטל את המצות שעל הקערה ומברך

בָּרוּךְ אַתָּה יְיָ, אֱלֹהֵינוּ מֶלֶךְ הָעוֹלָם, הַמּוֹצִיא לֶחֶם מִן הָאָרֶץ:

מניח את המצה התחתונה ובעודו אוחז את העליונה ואת הפרוסה מברך

בָּרוּךְ אַתָּה יְיָ, אֱלֹהֵינוּ מֶלֶךְ הָעוֹלָם, אֲשֶׁר קִדְּשָׁנוּ בְּמִצְוֹתָיו וְצִוָּנוּ עַל אֲכִילַת מַצָּה:

אוכלים כשיעור שני זיתים מצה וטובלים במלח

४ מָרוֹר ৪

לוקח כזית מרור, טובלו בחרוסת ומברך ואוכלו

בָּרוּךְ אַתָּה יְיָ אֱלֹהֵינוּ מֶלֶךְ הָעוֹלָם, אֲשֶׁר קִדְּשָׁנוּ בְּמִצְוֹתָיו וְצִוָּנוּ עַל אֲכִילַת מָרוֹר:

४ כּוֹרֵךְ ৪

פורס כזית מהמצה השלישית וכזית מרור, טובלו בחרוסת, כורכים יחד ואוכלם בהסיבה ואומר

זֵכֶר לְמִקְדָּשׁ כְּהִלֵּל: כֵּן עָשָׂה הִלֵּל בִּזְמַן שֶׁבֵּית הַמִּקְדָּשׁ הָיָה קַיָּם. הָיָה כּוֹרֵךְ פֶּסַח מַצָּה וּמָרוֹר וְאוֹכֵל בְּיַחַד. לְקַיֵּם מַה שֶּׁנֶּאֱמַר: עַל־מַצּוֹת וּמְרוֹרִים יֹאכְלֻהוּ:

ও Rachtzah ৪
Washing hands for the meal

Wash the hands for the meal

Blessed are You, Hashem our God, King of the universe, Who has sanctified us with His commandments, and commanded us concerning the washing of the hands.

ও Motzi Matzoh ৪
Blessings over the matzoh

Blessed are You, Hashem our God, King of the universe, Who brings forth bread from the earth.

Blessed are You, Hashem our God, King of the universe, Who has sanctified us with His commandments, and commanded us concerning the eating of matzoh.

ও Marror ৪
Bitter herbs

Blessed are You, Hashem our God, King of the universe, Who has sanctified us with His commandments, and commanded us concerning the eating of the bitter herbs.

ও Korech ৪
Marror and matzoh sandwich dipped in Charoses

In commemoration of the *Bais Hamikdash* we do as Hillel did when the *Bais Hamikdash* was in existence; he combined matzoh and marror in a sandwich and ate them together, to fulfill what is written in the Torah: "They shall eat it with matzos and bitter herbs."

ॐ שֻׁלְחָן עוֹרֵךְ ॐ

ॐ צָפוּן ॐ

אוֹכְלִים אֶת הָאֲפִיקוֹמָן

ॐ בָּרֵךְ ॐ

בִּרְכַּת הַמָּזוֹן

שִׁיר הַמַּעֲלוֹת בְּשׁוּב יְיָ אֶת שִׁיבַת צִיּוֹן הָיִינוּ כְּחֹלְמִים: אָז יִמָּלֵא שְׂחוֹק פִּינוּ וּלְשׁוֹנֵנוּ רִנָּה אָז יֹאמְרוּ בַגּוֹיִם הִגְדִּיל יְיָ לַעֲשׂוֹת עִם אֵלֶּה: הִגְדִּיל יְיָ לַעֲשׂוֹת עִמָּנוּ הָיִינוּ שְׂמֵחִים: שׁוּבָה יְיָ אֶת שְׁבִיתֵנוּ כַּאֲפִיקִים בַּנֶּגֶב: הַזֹּרְעִים בְּדִמְעָה בְּרִנָּה יִקְצֹרוּ: הָלוֹךְ יֵלֵךְ וּבָכֹה נֹשֵׂא מֶשֶׁךְ הַזָּרַע בֹּא יָבֹא בְרִנָּה נֹשֵׂא אֲלֻמֹּתָיו:

הַמְזַמֵּן: רַבּוֹתַי נְבָרֵךְ!

הַמְסֻבִּין: יְהִי שֵׁם יְיָ מְבֹרָךְ מֵעַתָּה וְעַד עוֹלָם.

הַמְזַמֵּן: יְהִי שֵׁם יְיָ מְבֹרָךְ מֵעַתָּה וְעַד עוֹלָם. בִּרְשׁוּת מָרָנָן וְרַבָּנָן וְרַבּוֹתַי, נְבָרֵךְ (אֱלֹהֵינוּ) שֶׁאָכַלְנוּ מִשֶּׁלּוֹ.

הַמְסֻבִּין: בָּרוּךְ (אֱלֹהֵינוּ) שֶׁאָכַלְנוּ מִשֶּׁלּוֹ וּבְטוּבוֹ חָיִינוּ.

הַמְזַמֵּן: בָּרוּךְ (אֱלֹהֵינוּ) שֶׁאָכַלְנוּ מִשֶּׁלּוֹ וּבְטוּבוֹ חָיִינוּ.

בָּרוּךְ הוּא וּבָרוּךְ שְׁמוֹ:

בָּרוּךְ אַתָּה יְיָ, אֱלֹהֵינוּ מֶלֶךְ הָעוֹלָם, הַזָּן אֶת הָעוֹלָם כֻּלּוֹ בְּטוּבוֹ בְּחֵן בְּחֶסֶד וּבְרַחֲמִים הוּא נוֹתֵן לֶחֶם לְכָל בָּשָׂר כִּי לְעוֹלָם חַסְדּוֹ. וּבְטוּבוֹ הַגָּדוֹל תָּמִיד לֹא חָסַר לָנוּ, וְאַל יֶחְסַר לָנוּ מָזוֹן לְעוֹלָם וָעֶד. בַּעֲבוּר שְׁמוֹ הַגָּדוֹל, כִּי הוּא אֵל זָן וּמְפַרְנֵס לַכֹּל וּמֵטִיב לַכֹּל, וּמֵכִין מָזוֹן לְכָל בְּרִיּוֹתָיו אֲשֶׁר בָּרָא. בָּרוּךְ אַתָּה יְיָ, הַזָּן אֶת הַכֹּל:

ॐ **Shulchan Orech** ℃
Serve the meal

ॐ **Tzafun** ℃
Partaking of the Afikoman

ॐ **Barech** ℃
Grace after meals

A Song of Ascents. When Hashem brought the exiles back to Zion, we were like those who dream. Then our mouth was filled with laughter, and our tongue with glad song. Then it will be said among the nations: "Hashem has done great things for them." Hashem has done great things for us, and we rejoiced. Restore our captives, Hashem, like streams in the Negev. Those who sow in tears shall reap in joy. Though the farmer bears the measure of seed to the field in tears, he shall come home with joy, bearing his sheaves.

The word "our" in parentheses is added if a minyan is present.

Seder leader: Gentlemen, let us say grace.

Guests respond: Blessed is the Name of Hashem
from this time forth and forever.

Seder leader continues: Blessed is the Name of Hashem
from this time forth and forever.

With the permission of the distinguished people present,
let us now bless (our) God Whose food we have eaten.

Guests respond: Blessed be (our) God Whose food we have eaten
and through Whose goodness we live.

Seder leader: Blessed be (our) God Whose food we have eaten
and through Whose goodness we live.

All: Blessed is He and blessed is His Name

Blessed are You, Hashem our God, King of the universe, Who nourishes the whole world with grace, kindness and mercy. He gives food to all creatures, for His kindness endures forever. Through His great goodness we have never been in want; may we never be in want of sustenance forever. For His great Name's sake because He is the God Who nourishes and sustains all, does good to all, and prepares food for all His creatures which He has created. Blessed are You, Hashem, Who nourishes all.

נוֹדֶה לְךָ יְיָ אֱלֹהֵינוּ עַל שֶׁהִנְחַלְתָּ לַאֲבוֹתֵינוּ, אֶרֶץ חֶמְדָּה טוֹבָה וּרְחָבָה, וְעַל שֶׁהוֹצֵאתָנוּ יְיָ אֱלֹהֵינוּ מֵאֶרֶץ מִצְרַיִם, וּפְדִיתָנוּ, מִבֵּית עֲבָדִים, וְעַל בְּרִיתְךָ שֶׁחָתַמְתָּ בִּבְשָׂרֵנוּ, וְעַל תּוֹרָתְךָ שֶׁלִּמַּדְתָּנוּ, וְעַל חֻקֶּיךָ שֶׁהוֹדַעְתָּנוּ וְעַל חַיִּים חֵן וָחֶסֶד שֶׁחוֹנַנְתָּנוּ, וְעַל אֲכִילַת מָזוֹן שָׁאַתָּה זָן וּמְפַרְנֵס אוֹתָנוּ תָּמִיד, בְּכָל יוֹם וּבְכָל עֵת וּבְכָל שָׁעָה:

וְעַל הַכֹּל יְיָ אֱלֹהֵינוּ אֲנַחְנוּ מוֹדִים לָךְ, וּמְבָרְכִים אוֹתָךְ, יִתְבָּרַךְ שִׁמְךָ בְּפִי כָּל חַי תָּמִיד לְעוֹלָם וָעֶד. כַּכָּתוּב, וְאָכַלְתָּ וְשָׂבָעְתָּ, וּבֵרַכְתָּ אֶת יְיָ אֱלֹהֶיךָ עַל הָאָרֶץ הַטֹּבָה אֲשֶׁר נָתַן לָךְ. בָּרוּךְ אַתָּה יְיָ, עַל הָאָרֶץ וְעַל הַמָּזוֹן:

רַחֵם נָא יְיָ אֱלֹהֵינוּ, עַל יִשְׂרָאֵל עַמֶּךָ, וְעַל יְרוּשָׁלַיִם עִירֶךָ, וְעַל צִיּוֹן מִשְׁכַּן כְּבוֹדֶךָ, וְעַל מַלְכוּת בֵּית דָּוִד מְשִׁיחֶךָ, וְעַל הַבַּיִת הַגָּדוֹל וְהַקָּדוֹשׁ שֶׁנִּקְרָא שִׁמְךָ עָלָיו. אֱלֹהֵינוּ, אָבִינוּ, רְעֵנוּ, זוּנֵנוּ, פַּרְנְסֵנוּ, וְכַלְכְּלֵנוּ, וְהַרְוִיחֵנוּ, וְהַרְוַח לָנוּ יְיָ אֱלֹהֵינוּ מְהֵרָה מִכָּל צָרוֹתֵינוּ, וְנָא, אַל תַּצְרִיכֵנוּ יְיָ אֱלֹהֵינוּ, לֹא לִידֵי מַתְּנַת בָּשָׂר וָדָם, וְלֹא לִידֵי הַלְוָאָתָם. כִּי אִם לְיָדְךָ הַמְּלֵאָה, הַפְּתוּחָה, הַקְּדוֹשָׁה וְהָרְחָבָה, שֶׁלֹּא נֵבוֹשׁ וְלֹא נִכָּלֵם לְעוֹלָם וָעֶד:

(כשחל יום טוב בשבת)

רְצֵה וְהַחֲלִיצֵנוּ יְיָ אֱלֹהֵינוּ בְּמִצְוֹתֶיךָ וּבְמִצְוַת יוֹם הַשְּׁבִיעִי הַשַּׁבָּת הַגָּדוֹל וְהַקָּדוֹשׁ הַזֶּה. כִּי יוֹם זֶה גָּדוֹל וְקָדוֹשׁ הוּא לְפָנֶיךָ, לִשְׁבָּת בּוֹ וְלָנוּחַ בּוֹ בְּאַהֲבָה כְּמִצְוַת רְצוֹנֶךָ וּבִרְצוֹנְךָ הָנִיחַ לָנוּ יְיָ אֱלֹהֵינוּ, שֶׁלֹּא תְהֵא צָרָה וְיָגוֹן וַאֲנָחָה בְּיוֹם מְנוּחָתֵנוּ. וְהַרְאֵנוּ יְיָ אֱלֹהֵינוּ בְּנֶחָמַת צִיּוֹן עִירֶךָ, וּבְבִנְיַן יְרוּשָׁלַיִם עִיר קָדְשֶׁךָ, כִּי אַתָּה הוּא בַּעַל הַיְשׁוּעוֹת וּבַעַל הַנֶּחָמוֹת:

אֱלֹהֵינוּ וֵאלֹהֵי אֲבוֹתֵינוּ, יַעֲלֶה וְיָבֹא וְיַגִּיעַ, וְיֵרָאֶה, וְיֵרָצֶה, וְיִשָּׁמַע, וְיִפָּקֵד, וְיִזָּכֵר זִכְרוֹנֵנוּ וּפִקְדוֹנֵנוּ, וְזִכְרוֹן אֲבוֹתֵינוּ, וְזִכְרוֹן מָשִׁיחַ בֶּן דָּוִד עַבְדֶּךָ, וְזִכְרוֹן יְרוּשָׁלַיִם עִיר קָדְשֶׁךָ, וְזִכְרוֹן כָּל עַמְּךָ בֵּית יִשְׂרָאֵל לְפָנֶיךָ, לִפְלֵיטָה לְטוֹבָה לְחֵן וּלְחֶסֶד וּלְרַחֲמִים, לְחַיִּים וּלְשָׁלוֹם בְּיוֹם חַג הַמַּצּוֹת הַזֶּה. זָכְרֵנוּ יְיָ אֱלֹהֵינוּ בּוֹ

We thank You, Hashem our God, for having given to our fathers as a heritage a beautiful, good, and spacious land; and for having taken us out, Hashem our God, from the land of Egypt and You redeemed us from the house of slavery; for Your covenant which You have sealed in our flesh; for Your Torah which You have taught us; for Your statutes which You have made known to us; for the life, grace and kindness You have bestowed on us; and for the provision of food with which You nourish and sustain us at all times—every day, every season and every hour.

For everything, Hashem our God, we thank You and bless You. May Your Name constantly be blessed by all forever, as it is written: " And you shall eat and be satisfied, and bless Hashem, Your God, for the good land He gave you." Blessed are You, Hashem, for the land and the food.

Have mercy, Hashem our God, on Yisrael Your people, on Jerusalem Your city, on Zion the abode of Your glory, on the kingdom of the house of David, Your anointed one, and on the great and holy *Bais Hamikdash* that bears Your Name. Our God, our Father, tend and nourish us; sustain and support us and relieve us. Speedily, Hashem our God, grant us relief from all our troubles. Hashem our God, make us not rely on the gifts and loans of men but rather on Your full, open, holy and generous hand, that we may never be put to shame and disgrace for ever.

On Sabbath add following paragraph:

Favor us and strengthen us, Hashem our God, with Your commandments-with the commandment concerning the seventh day, this great and holy Sabbath. This day is great and holy before You to abstain from work and rest on it in love according to Your will. In Your will, Hashem our God, grant us rest so that there be no sorrow grief and lament on our day of rest. And show us, Hashem our God, the consolation of Zion Your city, Jerusalem Your holy city rebuilt, for You are Master of all salvation and Master of consolation.

Our God and God of our fathers, may there ascend, come, reach, appear, be favored, be heard, and be remembered before You the remembrance of us, the remembrance of our fathers, the remembrance of *Moshiach* son of David, Your servant, the remembrance of Jerusalem Your holy city, and the remembrance of all Your people the house of Yisrael, for deliverance, for good, for grace, for kindness and for mercy, for life and for peace, on this day of the Feast of Matzos. Remember us on it, Hashem

לְטוֹבָה. וּפָקְדֵנוּ בוֹ לִבְרָכָה. וְהוֹשִׁיעֵנוּ בוֹ לְחַיִּים, וּבִדְבַר יְשׁוּעָה וְרַחֲמִים, חוּס וְחָנֵּנוּ, וְרַחֵם עָלֵינוּ וְהוֹשִׁיעֵנוּ, כִּי אֵלֶיךָ עֵינֵינוּ, כִּי אֵל מֶלֶךְ חַנּוּן וְרַחוּם אָתָּה:

וּבְנֵה יְרוּשָׁלַיִם עִיר הַקֹּדֶשׁ בִּמְהֵרָה בְיָמֵינוּ. בָּרוּךְ אַתָּה יְיָ, בּוֹנֶה בְרַחֲמָיו יְרוּשָׁלָיִם. אָמֵן

בָּרוּךְ: אַתָּה יְיָ אֱלֹהֵינוּ מֶלֶךְ הָעוֹלָם, הָאֵל אָבִינוּ, מַלְכֵּנוּ, אַדִּירֵנוּ בּוֹרְאֵנוּ, גּוֹאֲלֵנוּ, יוֹצְרֵנוּ, קְדוֹשֵׁנוּ קְדוֹשׁ יַעֲקֹב, רוֹעֵנוּ רוֹעֵה יִשְׂרָאֵל. הַמֶּלֶךְ הַטּוֹב, וְהַמֵּטִיב לַכֹּל, שֶׁבְּכָל יוֹם וָיוֹם הוּא הֵטִיב, הוּא מֵטִיב, הוּא יֵיטִיב לָנוּ. הוּא גְמָלָנוּ, הוּא גוֹמְלֵנוּ, הוּא יִגְמְלֵנוּ לָעַד לְחֵן וּלְחֶסֶד וּלְרַחֲמִים וּלְרֶוַח הַצָּלָה וְהַצְלָחָה בְּרָכָה וִישׁוּעָה, נֶחָמָה, פַּרְנָסָה וְכַלְכָּלָה, וְרַחֲמִים, וְחַיִּים וְשָׁלוֹם, וְכָל טוֹב, וּמִכָּל טוּב לְעוֹלָם אַל יְחַסְּרֵנוּ:

הָרַחֲמָן, הוּא יִמְלוֹךְ עָלֵינוּ לְעוֹלָם וָעֶד. הָרַחֲמָן, הוּא יִתְבָּרַךְ בַּשָּׁמַיִם וּבָאָרֶץ. הָרַחֲמָן, הוּא יִשְׁתַּבַּח לְדוֹר דּוֹרִים, וְיִתְפָּאַר בָּנוּ לָעַד וּלְנֵצַח נְצָחִים, וְיִתְהַדַּר בָּנוּ לָעַד וּלְעוֹלְמֵי עוֹלָמִים. הָרַחֲמָן, הוּא יְפַרְנְסֵנוּ בְּכָבוֹד. הָרַחֲמָן, הוּא יִשְׁבּוֹר עֻלֵּנוּ מֵעַל צַוָּארֵנוּ וְהוּא יוֹלִיכֵנוּ קוֹמְמִיּוּת לְאַרְצֵנוּ. הָרַחֲמָן, הוּא יִשְׁלַח לָנוּ בְּרָכָה מְרֻבָּה בַּבַּיִת הַזֶּה, וְעַל שֻׁלְחָן זֶה שֶׁאָכַלְנוּ עָלָיו. הָרַחֲמָן, הוּא יִשְׁלַח לָנוּ אֶת אֵלִיָּהוּ הַנָּבִיא זָכוּר לַטּוֹב, וִיבַשֵּׂר לָנוּ בְּשׂוֹרוֹת טוֹבוֹת יְשׁוּעוֹת וְנֶחָמוֹת.

הָרַחֲמָן, הוּא יְבָרֵךְ אֶת (אָבִי מוֹרִי) בַּעַל הַבַּיִת הַזֶּה, וְאֶת (אִמִּי מוֹרָתִי) בַּעֲלַת הַבַּיִת הַזֶּה,

הָרַחֲמָן, הוּא יְבָרֵךְ אוֹתִי (וְאֶת אָבִי וְאִמִּי וְאִשְׁתִּי וְזַרְעִי) וְאֶת כָּל אֲשֶׁר לִי

הָרַחֲמָן, הוּא יְבָרֵךְ אֶת בַּעַל הַבַּיִת הַזֶּה, וְאֶת אִשְׁתּוֹ בַּעֲלַת הַבַּיִת הַזֶּה.

אוֹתָם וְאֶת בֵּיתָם וְאֶת זַרְעָם וְאֶת כָּל אֲשֶׁר לָהֶם אוֹתָנוּ וְאֶת כָּל אֲשֶׁר לָנוּ, כְּמוֹ שֶׁנִּתְבָּרְכוּ אֲבוֹתֵינוּ, אַבְרָהָם יִצְחָק וְיַעֲקֹב: בַּכֹּל, מִכֹּל, כֹּל, כֵּן יְבָרֵךְ אוֹתָנוּ כֻּלָּנוּ יַחַד בִּבְרָכָה שְׁלֵמָה, וְנֹאמַר אָמֵן:

our God, for goodness; consider us on it for blessing; and save us on it for life. And in the matter of salvation and mercy spare us and favor us; have pity on us and save us, for we look to You, for You are a gracious and merciful God.

Rebuild Jerusalem the holy city speedily in our days. Blessed are You, Hashem, Who rebuilds Jerusalem in His mercy. Amen.

Blessed are You, Hashem our God, King of the universe. God You are our Father, our King and Sovereign, our Creator, our Redeemer, our Maker, our Holy One, Holy One of Yaakov, our Shepherd, the Shepherd of Yisrael, the good and beneficent King. Every single day He did good, He does good and will do good for us. He rewarded us, rewards us, and will forever reward us with grace, kindness and mercy, relief and deliverance, success, blessing, salvation, comfort, sustenance, support, mercy, life and peace and all goodness. May You never deprive us of any good thing.

May the Merciful One reign over us forever and ever. May the Merciful One be blessed in heaven and on earth. May the Merciful One be praised for all generations; may He be glorified through us forever and ever; may He be honored through us to all eternity. May the Merciful One grant us an honorable livelihood. May the Merciful One break the yoke of oppression from our necks and may He lead us upstanding into our land. May the Merciful One send ample blessing into this house and upon this table at which we have eaten. May the Merciful One send us Eliyahu Hanavi remembered for good to bring us good tidings, salvations and comfort.

At parents' table, add words in parenthesis:
May the Merciful One bless (my revered father) the master of this house and (my revered mother) the mistress of this house.

At own table, add:
May the Merciful One bless myself (my father and mother, my wife/ my husband and children) and all that belongs to me.

May the Merciful One bless the master of this house and the mistress of this house.

Them, their house, their offspring and all that is theirs, just as our forefathers Avraham, Yitzchak, and Yaakov were blessed in everything, from everything, with everything. Thus may He bless all of us together with a perfect blessing, and let us say, Amen.

בַּמָּרוֹם יְלַמְּדוּ עֲלֵיהֶם וְעָלֵינוּ זְכוּת, שֶׁתְּהֵא לְמִשְׁמֶרֶת שָׁלוֹם, וְנִשָּׂא בְרָכָה מֵאֵת יְיָ וּצְדָקָה מֵאֱלֹהֵי יִשְׁעֵנוּ, וְנִמְצָא חֵן וְשֵׂכֶל טוֹב בְּעֵינֵי אֱלֹהִים וְאָדָם:

לשבת

הָרַחֲמָן, הוּא יַנְחִילֵנוּ יוֹם שֶׁכֻּלּוֹ שַׁבָּת וּמְנוּחָה לְחַיֵּי הָעוֹלָמִים.

הָרַחֲמָן, הוּא יַנְחִילֵנוּ יוֹם שֶׁכֻּלּוֹ טוֹב.

הָרַחֲמָן, הוּא יְזַכֵּנוּ לִימוֹת הַמָּשִׁיחַ וּלְחַיֵּי הָעוֹלָם הַבָּא.

מִגְדּוֹל יְשׁוּעוֹת מַלְכּוֹ, וְעֹשֶׂה חֶסֶד לִמְשִׁיחוֹ לְדָוִד וּלְזַרְעוֹ עַד עוֹלָם: עֹשֶׂה שָׁלוֹם בִּמְרוֹמָיו, הוּא יַעֲשֶׂה שָׁלוֹם, עָלֵינוּ וְעַל כָּל יִשְׂרָאֵל, וְאִמְרוּ אָמֵן:

יְראוּ אֶת יְיָ קְדֹשָׁיו, כִּי אֵין מַחְסוֹר לִירֵאָיו: כְּפִירִים רָשׁוּ וְרָעֵבוּ, וְדוֹרְשֵׁי יְיָ לֹא יַחְסְרוּ כָל טוֹב: הוֹדוּ לַיְיָ כִּי טוֹב, כִּי לְעוֹלָם חַסְדּוֹ: פּוֹתֵחַ אֶת יָדֶךָ, וּמַשְׂבִּיעַ לְכָל חַי רָצוֹן: בָּרוּךְ הַגֶּבֶר אֲשֶׁר יִבְטַח בַּיְיָ, וְהָיָה יְיָ מִבְטַחוֹ: נַעַר הָיִיתִי גַם זָקַנְתִּי וְלֹא רָאִיתִי צַדִּיק נֶעֱזָב, וְזַרְעוֹ מְבַקֶּשׁ לָחֶם: יְיָ עֹז לְעַמּוֹ יִתֵּן, יְיָ יְבָרֵךְ אֶת עַמּוֹ בַשָּׁלוֹם:

כוס שלישית

בָּרוּךְ אַתָּה יְיָ, אֱלֹהֵינוּ מֶלֶךְ הָעוֹלָם, בּוֹרֵא פְּרִי הַגָּפֶן:

מוזגים כוס מיוחדת לאליהו הנביא, ופותחים את הדלת ואומרים

שְׁפֹךְ חֲמָתְךָ אֶל הַגּוֹיִם, אֲשֶׁר לֹא יְדָעוּךָ וְעַל מַמְלָכוֹת אֲשֶׁר בְּשִׁמְךָ לֹא קָרָאוּ: כִּי אָכַל אֶת יַעֲקֹב. וְאֶת נָוֵהוּ הֵשַׁמּוּ: שְׁפָךְ עֲלֵיהֶם זַעֲמֶךָ, וַחֲרוֹן אַפְּךָ יַשִּׂיגֵם: תִּרְדֹּף בְּאַף וְתַשְׁמִידֵם, מִתַּחַת שְׁמֵי יְיָ:

On high may they and we find merit for a preservation of peace. May we receive a blessing from Hashem, justice from the God of our salvation, and may we find favor and intelligence in the eyes of God and man.

On Sabbath add
May the Merciful One cause us to inherit the day which will be a complete Sabbath and rest for the eternal life.

On Seder night add
May the Merciful One cause us to inherit the day of total goodness.

May the Merciful One make us worthy to live in the days of *Moshiach* and the life of the world to come. He is the tower of salvation to His king and shows kindness to His anointed, to David and his descendants forever. He Who creates peace in His heavenly heights, may He grant peace for us and for all Yisrael; and say, Amen.

Revere Hashem, you His holy ones for those who revere Him suffer no want. Young lions may be wanting and starving, but those who seek Hashem shall not lack any good thing. Give thanks to Hashem, for He is good; His kindness endures forever. You open Your hand and satisfy the desire of every living thing. Blessed is the man who trusts in Hashem, and Hashem is his trust. I was a youth and now I am old, but never have I seen the righteous man forsaken, nor his children begging for bread. Hashem will give strength to His nation; Hashem will bless His nation with peace.

Over the third cup of wine, say:
Blessed are You, Hashem our God, King of the universe, Who creates the fruit of the vine.

A cup of wine is poured in honor of Eliyahu Hanavi. The door is opened and the Hallel continues, introduced by the paragraph 'Shfoch Chamascha'.
Pour out Your rage upon the nations that do not know You, and upon the kingdoms that do not invoke Your Name. For they have consumed Yaakov, and destroyed His Sanctuary. Pour Your anger upon them and let the fire of Your wrath overtake them. Pursue them with wrath and destroy them from under the Heavens of Hashem.

❧ הַלֵּל ❧

לֹא לָנוּ יְיָ לֹא לָנוּ כִּי לְשִׁמְךָ תֵּן כָּבוֹד, עַל חַסְדְּךָ עַל אֲמִתֶּךָ. לָמָּה יֹאמְרוּ הַגּוֹיִם, אַיֵּה נָא אֱלֹהֵיהֶם. וֵאלֹהֵינוּ בַשָּׁמָיִם כֹּל אֲשֶׁר חָפֵץ עָשָׂה. עֲצַבֵּיהֶם כֶּסֶף וְזָהָב, מַעֲשֵׂה יְדֵי אָדָם. פֶּה לָהֶם וְלֹא יְדַבֵּרוּ, עֵינַיִם לָהֶם וְלֹא יִרְאוּ. אָזְנַיִם לָהֶם וְלֹא יִשְׁמָעוּ, אַף לָהֶם וְלֹא יְרִיחוּן. יְדֵיהֶם וְלֹא יְמִישׁוּן, רַגְלֵיהֶם וְלֹא יְהַלֵּכוּ, לֹא יֶהְגּוּ בִּגְרוֹנָם. כְּמוֹהֶם יִהְיוּ עֹשֵׂיהֶם, כֹּל אֲשֶׁר בֹּטֵחַ בָּהֶם: יִשְׂרָאֵל בְּטַח בַּיְיָ, עֶזְרָם וּמָגִנָּם הוּא. בֵּית אַהֲרֹן בִּטְחוּ בַיְיָ, עֶזְרָם וּמָגִנָּם הוּא. יִרְאֵי יְיָ בִּטְחוּ בַיְיָ, עֶזְרָם וּמָגִנָּם הוּא:

יְיָ זְכָרָנוּ יְבָרֵךְ, יְבָרֵךְ אֶת בֵּית יִשְׂרָאֵל, יְבָרֵךְ אֶת בֵּית אַהֲרֹן. יְבָרֵךְ יִרְאֵי יְיָ, הַקְּטַנִּים עִם הַגְּדֹלִים. יֹסֵף יְיָ עֲלֵיכֶם, עֲלֵיכֶם וְעַל בְּנֵיכֶם. בְּרוּכִים אַתֶּם לַיְיָ, עֹשֵׂה שָׁמַיִם וָאָרֶץ. הַשָּׁמַיִם שָׁמַיִם לַיְיָ, וְהָאָרֶץ נָתַן לִבְנֵי אָדָם. לֹא הַמֵּתִים יְהַלְלוּ יָהּ, וְלֹא כָּל יֹרְדֵי דוּמָה. וַאֲנַחְנוּ נְבָרֵךְ יָהּ, מֵעַתָּה וְעַד עוֹלָם, הַלְלוּיָהּ:

אָהַבְתִּי כִּי יִשְׁמַע יְיָ, אֶת קוֹלִי תַּחֲנוּנָי. כִּי הִטָּה אָזְנוֹ לִי וּבְיָמַי אֶקְרָא: אֲפָפוּנִי חֶבְלֵי מָוֶת, וּמְצָרֵי שְׁאוֹל מְצָאוּנִי צָרָה וְיָגוֹן אֶמְצָא. וּבְשֵׁם יְיָ אֶקְרָא, אָנָּה יְיָ מַלְּטָה נַפְשִׁי. חַנּוּן יְיָ וְצַדִּיק, וֵאלֹהֵינוּ מְרַחֵם. שֹׁמֵר פְּתָאיִם יְיָ דַּלּוֹתִי וְלִי יְהוֹשִׁיעַ. שׁוּבִי נַפְשִׁי לִמְנוּחָיְכִי, כִּי יְיָ גָּמַל עָלָיְכִי. כִּי חִלַּצְתָּ נַפְשִׁי מִמָּוֶת אֶת עֵינִי מִן דִּמְעָה, אֶת רַגְלִי מִדֶּחִי. אֶתְהַלֵּךְ לִפְנֵי יְיָ, בְּאַרְצוֹת הַחַיִּים. הֶאֱמַנְתִּי כִּי אֲדַבֵּר, אֲנִי עָנִיתִי מְאֹד. אֲנִי אָמַרְתִּי בְחָפְזִי כָּל הָאָדָם כֹּזֵב.

מָה אָשִׁיב לַיְיָ, כָּל תַּגְמוּלוֹהִי עָלָי. כּוֹס יְשׁוּעוֹת אֶשָּׂא, וּבְשֵׁם יְיָ אֶקְרָא. נְדָרַי לַיְיָ אֲשַׁלֵּם, נֶגְדָה נָּא לְכָל עַמּוֹ. יָקָר בְּעֵינֵי יְיָ הַמָּוְתָה לַחֲסִידָיו. אָנָּה יְיָ כִּי אֲנִי עַבְדֶּךָ אֲנִי עַבְדְּךָ, בֶּן אֲמָתֶךָ פִּתַּחְתָּ לְמוֹסֵרָי. לְךָ אֶזְבַּח זֶבַח תּוֹדָה וּבְשֵׁם יְיָ אֶקְרָא. נְדָרַי לַיְיָ אֲשַׁלֵּם נֶגְדָה נָּא לְכָל עַמּוֹ. בְּחַצְרוֹת בֵּית יְיָ בְּתוֹכֵכִי יְרוּשָׁלָיִם הַלְלוּיָהּ:

ೞ Hallel ೞ
Reciting the Hallel

Not for our sake, Hashem, not for our sake, but for Your Name's sake give glory, because of Your kindness and Your truth. Why should the nations say: "Where is their God?" Our God is in the heavens; He does whatever He pleases! Their idols are silver and gold, the work of human hands. They have a mouth, but they cannot speak; they have eyes, but they cannot see; they have ears, but they cannot hear; they have a nose, but they cannot smell; they have hands, but they cannot feel; they have feet, but they cannot walk; nor can they utter a sound with their throat. Those who make them shall become like them, whoever trusts in them. Yisrael, trust in Hashem! He is their help and their shield. House of Aharon, trust in Hashem! He is their help and their shield. You who revere Hashem, trust in Hashem! He is their help and their shield.

Hashem Who has remembered us will bless; He will bless the house of Yisrael; He will bless the house of Aharon; He will bless those who revere Hashem, the small with the great. May Hashem increase you, you and your children. You are blessed by Hashem, Who made the heaven and earth. The heaven is Hashem's heaven, but He has given the earth to mankind. The dead cannot praise Hashem, nor can any who go down into silence. We will bless Hashem from this time forth and forever. Halleluyah!

I love that Hashem hears my voice, my supplications. Because He has inclined His ear to me, I will call upon Him as long as I live. The cords of death encircled me; the confines of the grave have overtaken me; I found trouble and sorrow. Then I called upon the Name of Hashem: "Please Hashem, save my life!" Gracious is Hashem, and righteous and our God is merciful. Hashem protects the simple; I was brought low and He saved me. Return to your rest, my soul, for Hashem has been kind to you. You have delivered my soul from death, my eyes from tears and my feet from stumbling. I shall walk before Hashem in the lands of the living. I kept faith even when I cry out: "I am greatly afflicted." [I kept faith even when] I said in haste: "All men are deceitful."

How can I repay Hashem for all His kind acts toward me? I will raise the cup of salvations, and call upon the Name of Hashem. My vows to Hashem I will pay in the presence of all His people. Precious in the sight of Hashem is the death of His pious ones. Please, Hashem, I am truly Your servant; I am Your servant, the son of Your maid; You have loosened my bonds. To You I sacrifice a thanksgiving offering, and call upon the Name of Hashem. My vows to Hashem I will pay in the presence of all His people, in the courtyards of Hashem's house, in your midst, Jerusalem. Halleluyah!

הַלְלוּ אֶת יְיָ, כָּל גּוֹיִם, שַׁבְּחוּהוּ כָּל הָאֻמִּים. כִּי גָבַר עָלֵינוּ חַסְדּוֹ, וֶאֱמֶת יְיָ לְעוֹלָם הַלְלוּיָהּ:

הוֹדוּ לַיְיָ כִּי טוֹב, כִּי לְעוֹלָם חַסְדּוֹ:

יֹאמַר נָא יִשְׂרָאֵל, כִּי לְעוֹלָם חַסְדּוֹ:

יֹאמְרוּ נָא בֵית אַהֲרֹן, כִּי לְעוֹלָם חַסְדּוֹ:

יֹאמְרוּ נָא יִרְאֵי יְיָ, כִּי לְעוֹלָם חַסְדּוֹ:

מִן הַמֵּצַר קָרָאתִי יָהּ, עָנָנִי בַמֶּרְחָב יָהּ. יְיָ לִי לֹא אִירָא, מַה יַּעֲשֶׂה לִי אָדָם. יְיָ לִי בְּעֹזְרָי, וַאֲנִי אֶרְאֶה בְשֹׂנְאָי. טוֹב לַחֲסוֹת בַּיְיָ, מִבְּטֹחַ בָּאָדָם. טוֹב לַחֲסוֹת בַּיְיָ מִבְּטֹחַ בִּנְדִיבִים. כָּל גּוֹיִם סְבָבוּנִי בְּשֵׁם יְיָ כִּי אֲמִילַם. סַבּוּנִי גַם סְבָבוּנִי בְּשֵׁם יְיָ כִּי אֲמִילַם. סַבּוּנִי כִדְבֹרִים דֹעֲכוּ כְּאֵשׁ קוֹצִים, בְּשֵׁם יְיָ כִּי אֲמִילַם. דָּחֹה דְחִיתַנִי לִנְפֹּל, וַיְיָ עֲזָרָנִי. עָזִּי וְזִמְרָת יָהּ, וַיְהִי לִי לִישׁוּעָה. קוֹל רִנָּה וִישׁוּעָה בְּאָהֳלֵי צַדִּיקִים, יְמִין יְיָ עֹשָׂה חָיִל. יְמִין יְיָ רוֹמֵמָה, יְמִין יְיָ עֹשָׂה חָיִל. לֹא אָמוּת כִּי אֶחְיֶה, וַאֲסַפֵּר מַעֲשֵׂי יָהּ. יַסֹּר יִסְּרַנִּי יָּהּ, וְלַמָּוֶת לֹא נְתָנָנִי. פִּתְחוּ לִי שַׁעֲרֵי צֶדֶק ,אָבֹא בָם אוֹדֶה יָהּ. זֶה הַשַּׁעַר לַיְיָ, צַדִּיקִים יָבֹאוּ בוֹ. אוֹדְךָ כִּי עֲנִיתָנִי, וַתְּהִי לִי לִישׁוּעָה. אוֹדְךָ כִּי עֲנִיתָנִי וַתְּהִי לִי לִישׁוּעָה. אֶבֶן מָאֲסוּ הַבּוֹנִים, הָיְתָה לְרֹאשׁ פִּנָּה. אֶבֶן מָאֲסוּ הַבּוֹנִים, הָיְתָה לְרֹאשׁ פִּנָּה. מֵאֵת יְיָ הָיְתָה זֹּאת, הִיא נִפְלָאת בְּעֵינֵינוּ: מֵאֵת יְיָ הָיְתָה זֹּאת, הִיא נִפְלָאת בְּעֵינֵינוּ. זֶה הַיּוֹם עָשָׂה יְיָ, נָגִילָה וְנִשְׂמְחָה בוֹ. זֶה הַיּוֹם עָשָׂה יְיָ נָגִילָה וְנִשְׂמְחָה בוֹ.

אָנָּא יְיָ הוֹשִׁיעָה נָּא: אָנָּא יְיָ הוֹשִׁיעָה נָּא:

אָנָּא יְיָ הַצְלִיחָה נָּא: אָנָּא יְיָ הַצְלִיחָה נָּא:

Praise Hashem, all you nations; praise Him, all you peoples! For His kindness overwhelms us, and the truth of Hashem is forever, Halleluyah!

Give thanks to Hashem, for He is good; His kindness endures forever.
Let Yisrael say: His kindness endures forever.
Let the house of Aharon say: His kindness endures forever.
Let those who revere Hashem say: His kindness endures forever.

Out of distress I called to Hashem; Hashem answered me with expansiveness. Hashem is with me; I have no fear of what man can do to me. Hashem is with me through my helpers; therefore I can face my enemies. It is better to seek refuge in Hashem than to trust in man. It is better to seek refuge in Hashem than to trust in princes. All nations have encompassed me; but in the Name of Hashem, I routed them. They swarmed around me; but in the Name of Hashem, I cut them down. They swarmed like bees about me, but they were extinguished like a fire does thorns; in the Name of Hashem, I cut them down. You pushed me hard that I might fall, but Hashem helped me. Hashem is my strength and song; He has become my salvation. The voice of rejoicing and salvation is (heard) in the tents of the righteous: "The right hand of Hashem does valiantly. Hashem's right hand is raised in triumph; Hashem's right hand does valiantly!" I shall not die, but live to relate the deeds of Hashem. Hashem has surely punished me, but He has not let me die. Open for me the gates of righteousness, that I may enter and thank Hashem. This is the gate of Hashem; the righteous may enter through it. I thank You for You have answered me and have become my salvation. I thank You for You have answered me and have become my salvation. The stone which the builders rejected has become the cornerstone. The stone which the builders rejected has become the cornerstone. This has come forth from Hashem; It is marvelous in our eyes. This has come forth from Hashem; It is marvelous in our eyes. This is the day which Hashem has made; We will be glad and rejoice on it. This is the day which Hashem has made; We will be glad and rejoice on it.

Hashem, please save us! Hashem, please save us!
Hashem, please let us prosper! Hashem, please let us prosper!

בָּרוּךְ הַבָּא בְּשֵׁם יְיָ, בֵּרַכְנוּכֶם מִבֵּית יְיָ. בָּרוּךְ הַבָּא בְּשֵׁם יְיָ, בֵּרַכְנוּכֶם מִבֵּית יְיָ. אֵל יְיָ וַיָּאֶר לָנוּ, אִסְרוּ חַג בַּעֲבֹתִים עַד קַרְנוֹת הַמִּזְבֵּחַ. אֵל יְיָ וַיָּאֶר לָנוּ, אִסְרוּ חַג בַּעֲבֹתִים, עַד קַרְנוֹת הַמִּזְבֵּחַ. אֵלִי אַתָּה וְאוֹדֶךָּ אֱלֹהַי אֲרוֹמְמֶךָּ. אֵלִי אַתָּה וְאוֹדֶךָּ אֱלֹהַי אֲרוֹמְמֶךָּ: הוֹדוּ לַיְיָ כִּי טוֹב, כִּי לְעוֹלָם חַסְדּוֹ: הוֹדוּ לַיְיָ כִּי טוֹב, כִּי לְעוֹלָם חַסְדּוֹ.

יְהַלְלוּךָ יְיָ אֱלֹהֵינוּ כָּל מַעֲשֶׂיךָ, וַחֲסִידֶיךָ צַדִּיקִים עוֹשֵׂי רְצוֹנֶךָ, וְכָל עַמְּךָ בֵּית יִשְׂרָאֵל בְּרִנָּה יוֹדוּ וִיבָרְכוּ וִישַׁבְּחוּ וִיפָאֲרוּ וִירוֹמְמוּ וְיַעֲרִיצוּ וְיַקְדִּישׁוּ וְיַמְלִיכוּ אֶת שִׁמְךָ מַלְכֵּנוּ, כִּי לְךָ טוֹב לְהוֹדוֹת וּלְשִׁמְךָ נָאֶה לְזַמֵּר, כִּי מֵעוֹלָם וְעַד עוֹלָם אַתָּה אֵל.

הוֹדוּ לַיְיָ כִּי טוֹב, כִּי לְעוֹלָם חַסְדּוֹ:

הוֹדוּ לֵאלֹהֵי הָאֱלֹהִים, כִּי לְעוֹלָם חַסְדּוֹ:

הוֹדוּ לַאֲדֹנֵי הָאֲדֹנִים, כִּי לְעוֹלָם חַסְדּוֹ:

לְעֹשֵׂה נִפְלָאוֹת גְּדֹלוֹת לְבַדּוֹ, כִּי לְעוֹלָם חַסְדּוֹ:

לְעֹשֵׂה הַשָּׁמַיִם בִּתְבוּנָה, כִּי לְעוֹלָם חַסְדּוֹ:

לְרוֹקַע הָאָרֶץ עַל הַמָּיִם, כִּי לְעוֹלָם חַסְדּוֹ:

לְעֹשֵׂה אוֹרִים גְּדֹלִים, כִּי לְעוֹלָם חַסְדּוֹ:

אֶת הַשֶּׁמֶשׁ לְמֶמְשֶׁלֶת בַּיּוֹם, כִּי לְעוֹלָם חַסְדּוֹ:

אֶת הַיָּרֵחַ וְכוֹכָבִים לְמֶמְשְׁלוֹת בַּלַּיְלָה, כִּי לְעוֹלָם חַסְדּוֹ:

לְמַכֵּה מִצְרַיִם בִּבְכוֹרֵיהֶם, כִּי לְעוֹלָם חַסְדּוֹ:

וַיּוֹצֵא יִשְׂרָאֵל מִתּוֹכָם, כִּי לְעוֹלָם חַסְדּוֹ:

בְּיָד חֲזָקָה וּבִזְרוֹעַ נְטוּיָה, כִּי לְעוֹלָם חַסְדּוֹ:

לְגֹזֵר יַם סוּף לִגְזָרִים, כִּי לְעוֹלָם חַסְדּוֹ:

Blessed be he who comes in the Name of Hashem; we bless you from the house of Hashem. Blessed be he who comes in the Name of Hashem; we bless you from the house of Hashem. Hashem is God Who has shown us light; Bind the sacrifice with cords, up to the altar-horns. Hashem is God Who has shown us light; Bind the sacrifice with cords, up to the altar-horns. You are my God, and I thank You; You are my God, and I exalt You. You are my God, and I thank You; You are my God, and I exalt You. Give thanks to Hashem, for He is good; His kindness endures forever. Give thanks to Hashem, for He is good; His kindness endures forever.

All Your works praise You, Hashem our God; Your pious ones, the righteous who perform Your will, and all Your people the House of Yisrael, with joy will thank, bless, praise, glorify, exalt, revere, sanctify, and coronate Your Name, our King. To You it is fitting to give thanks, and unto Your Name it is proper to sing praises, for You are God eternal.

Give thanks to Hashem, for He is good, His kindness endures forever;

Give thanks to the God of gods, His kindness endures forever;

Give thanks to Lord of lords, His kindness endures forever;

To Him Who alone does great wonders, His kindness endures forever;

To Him Who made the heavens with understanding,
His kindness endures forever;

To Him Who stretched the earth over the waters,
His kindness endures forever;

To Him Who made the great lights, His kindness endures forever;

The sun to reign by day, His kindness endures forever;

The moon and the stars to reign by night, His kindness endures forever;

To Him Who smote Egypt through their firstborn,
His kindness endures forever;

And took Yisrael out from among them, His kindness endures forever;

With strong hand and outstretched arm, His kindness endures forever;

To Him Who divided the Red Sea into parts,
His kindness endures forever;

וְהֶעֱבִיר יִשְׂרָאֵל בְּתוֹכוֹ, כִּי לְעוֹלָם חַסְדּוֹ:

וְנִעֵר פַּרְעֹה וְחֵילוֹ בְיַם סוּף, כִּי לְעוֹלָם חַסְדּוֹ:

לְמוֹלִיךְ עַמּוֹ בַּמִּדְבָּר, כִּי לְעוֹלָם חַסְדּוֹ:

לְמַכֵּה מְלָכִים גְּדֹלִים, כִּי לְעוֹלָם חַסְדּוֹ:

וַיַּהֲרֹג מְלָכִים אַדִּירִים, כִּי לְעוֹלָם חַסְדּוֹ:

לְסִיחוֹן מֶלֶךְ הָאֱמֹרִי, כִּי לְעוֹלָם חַסְדּוֹ:

וּלְעוֹג מֶלֶךְ הַבָּשָׁן, כִּי לְעוֹלָם חַסְדּוֹ:

וְנָתַן אַרְצָם לְנַחֲלָה, כִּי לְעוֹלָם חַסְדּוֹ:

נַחֲלָה לְיִשְׂרָאֵל עַבְדּוֹ, כִּי לְעוֹלָם חַסְדּוֹ:

שֶׁבְּשִׁפְלֵנוּ זָכַר לָנוּ, כִּי לְעוֹלָם חַסְדּוֹ:

וַיִּפְרְקֵנוּ מִצָּרֵינוּ, כִּי לְעוֹלָם חַסְדּוֹ:

נוֹתֵן לֶחֶם לְכָל בָּשָׂר, כִּי לְעוֹלָם חַסְדּוֹ:

הוֹדוּ לְאֵל הַשָּׁמָיִם, כִּי לְעוֹלָם חַסְדּוֹ:

נִשְׁמַת כָּל חַי, תְּבָרֵךְ אֶת שִׁמְךָ יְיָ אֱלֹהֵינוּ. וְרוּחַ כָּל בָּשָׂר, תְּפָאֵר וּתְרוֹמֵם זִכְרְךָ מַלְכֵּנוּ תָּמִיד, מִן הָעוֹלָם וְעַד הָעוֹלָם אַתָּה אֵל. וּמִבַּלְעָדֶיךָ אֵין לָנוּ מֶלֶךְ גּוֹאֵל וּמוֹשִׁיעַ, פּוֹדֶה וּמַצִּיל וּמְפַרְנֵס וּמְרַחֵם, בְּכָל עֵת צָרָה וְצוּקָה. אֵין לָנוּ מֶלֶךְ אֶלָּא אָתָּה: אֱלֹהֵי הָרִאשׁוֹנִים וְהָאַחֲרוֹנִים, אֱלוֹהַּ כָּל בְּרִיּוֹת, אֲדוֹן כָּל תּוֹלָדוֹת, הַמְהֻלָּל בְּרֹב הַתִּשְׁבָּחוֹת, הַמְנַהֵג עוֹלָמוֹ בְּחֶסֶד, וּבְרִיּוֹתָיו בְּרַחֲמִים. וַיְיָ לֹא יָנוּם וְלֹא יִישָׁן, הַמְעוֹרֵר יְשֵׁנִים וְהַמֵּקִיץ נִרְדָּמִים, וְהַמֵּשִׂיחַ אִלְּמִים, וְהַמַּתִּיר אֲסוּרִים, וְהַסּוֹמֵךְ נוֹפְלִים, וְהַזּוֹקֵף כְּפוּפִים, לְךָ לְבַדְּךָ אֲנַחְנוּ מוֹדִים. אִלּוּ פִינוּ מָלֵא שִׁירָה כַיָּם, וּלְשׁוֹנֵנוּ רִנָּה כַּהֲמוֹן גַּלָּיו, וְשִׂפְתוֹתֵינוּ שֶׁבַח כְּמֶרְחֲבֵי רָקִיעַ, וְעֵינֵינוּ מְאִירוֹת כַּשֶּׁמֶשׁ וְכַיָּרֵחַ, וְיָדֵינוּ פְרוּשׂוֹת כְּנִשְׁרֵי שָׁמָיִם, וְרַגְלֵינוּ קַלּוֹת כָּאַיָּלוֹת, אֵין אֲנַחְנוּ

And caused Yisrael to pass through it, His kindness endures forever;

And threw Pharaoh and his force in the Red Sea,
His kindness endures forever;

To Him Who led His people through the wilderness,
His kindness endures forever;

To Him Who smote great kings, His kindness endures forever;

And slew mighty kings, His kindness endures forever; Sichon, king
of the Amorites, His kindness endures forever; And Og, king of Bashan,
His kindness endures forever;

And gave their land as an inheritance, His kindness endures forever;

An inheritance to Yisrael His servant, His kindness endures forever;

Who remembered us in our low state, His kindness endures forever;

And released us from our foes, His kindness endures forever;

Who gives food to all creatures, His kindness endures forever;

Give thanks to God of heaven, His kindness endures forever.

The soul of every living being shall bless Your Name, Hashem our
God the spirit of all flesh shall ever glorify and exalt Your
remembrance, our King. Throughout eternity You are God. Besides
You we have no king Who redeems and saves, ransoms and rescues,
sustains and shows mercy in all times of trouble and distress. We
have no King but You—God of the first and of the last, God of all
creatures, Master of all generations, One acclaimed with a multitude
of praises, He Who guides His world with kindness and His creatures
with mercy. Hashem neither slumbers nor sleeps; He rouses those
who sleep and wakens those who slumber; He enables the speechless
to speak and loosens the bonds of the captives; He supports those
who are fallen and raises those who are bowed down. To You alone
we give thanks. Were our mouth as filled with song as the sea, and
our tongue with joy as the endless waves; were our lips full of
praise as the wide heavens, and our eyes shining like the sun or the
moon; were our hands spread out in prayer as the eagles of the
sky and our feet as swift as the deer—we would still be unable

מַסְפִּיקִים, לְהוֹדוֹת לְךָ יְיָ אֱלֹהֵינוּ וֵאלֹהֵי אֲבוֹתֵינוּ, וּלְבָרֵךְ אֶת שִׁמְךָ עַל אַחַת מֵאֶלֶף אַלְפֵי אֲלָפִים וְרִבֵּי רְבָבוֹת פְּעָמִים, הַטּוֹבוֹת שֶׁעָשִׂיתָ עִם אֲבוֹתֵינוּ וְעִמָּנוּ. מִמִּצְרַיִם גְּאַלְתָּנוּ יְיָ אֱלֹהֵינוּ, וּמִבֵּית עֲבָדִים פְּדִיתָנוּ, בְּרָעָב זַנְתָּנוּ, וּבְשָׂבָע כִּלְכַּלְתָּנוּ, מֵחֶרֶב הִצַּלְתָּנוּ, וּמִדֶּבֶר מִלַּטְתָּנוּ, וּמֵחֳלָיִם רָעִים וְנֶאֱמָנִים דִּלִּיתָנוּ: עַד הֵנָּה עֲזָרוּנוּ רַחֲמֶיךָ, וְלֹא עֲזָבוּנוּ חֲסָדֶיךָ וְאַל תִּטְּשֵׁנוּ יְיָ אֱלֹהֵינוּ לָנֶצַח. עַל כֵּן אֵבָרִים שֶׁפִּלַּגְתָּ בָּנוּ, וְרוּחַ וּנְשָׁמָה שֶׁנָּפַחְתָּ בְּאַפֵּינוּ, וְלָשׁוֹן אֲשֶׁר שַׂמְתָּ בְּפִינוּ, הֵן הֵם יוֹדוּ וִיבָרְכוּ וִישַׁבְּחוּ וִיפָאֲרוּ וִירוֹמְמוּ וְיַעֲרִיצוּ וְיַקְדִּישׁוּ וְיַמְלִיכוּ אֶת שִׁמְךָ מַלְכֵּנוּ, כִּי כָל פֶּה לְךָ יוֹדֶה, וְכָל לָשׁוֹן לְךָ תִשָּׁבַע, וְכָל בֶּרֶךְ לְךָ תִכְרַע, וְכָל קוֹמָה לְפָנֶיךָ תִשְׁתַּחֲוֶה, וְכָל לְבָבוֹת יִירָאוּךָ, וְכָל קֶרֶב וּכְלָיוֹת יְזַמְּרוּ לִשְׁמֶךָ. כַּדָּבָר שֶׁכָּתוּב, כָּל עַצְמוֹתַי תֹּאמַרְנָה יְיָ מִי כָמוֹךָ. מַצִּיל עָנִי מֵחָזָק מִמֶּנּוּ, וְעָנִי וְאֶבְיוֹן מִגֹּזְלוֹ: מִי יִדְמֶה לָּךְ, וּמִי יִשְׁוֶה לָּךְ וּמִי יַעֲרָךְ לָךְ: הָאֵל הַגָּדוֹל הַגִּבּוֹר וְהַנּוֹרָא, אֵל עֶלְיוֹן קֹנֵה שָׁמַיִם וָאָרֶץ: נְהַלֶּלְךָ וּנְשַׁבֵּחֲךָ וּנְפָאֶרְךָ וּנְבָרֵךְ אֶת־שֵׁם קָדְשֶׁךָ. כָּאָמוּר, לְדָוִד, בָּרְכִי נַפְשִׁי אֶת יְיָ, וְכָל קְרָבַי אֶת שֵׁם קָדְשׁוֹ:

הָאֵל בְּתַעֲצֻמוֹת עֻזֶּךָ, הַגָּדוֹל בִּכְבוֹד שְׁמֶךָ. הַגִּבּוֹר לָנֶצַח וְהַנּוֹרָא בְּנוֹרְאוֹתֶיךָ. הַמֶּלֶךְ הַיּוֹשֵׁב עַל כִּסֵּא רָם וְנִשָּׂא:

שׁוֹכֵן עַד, מָרוֹם וְקָדוֹשׁ שְׁמוֹ: וְכָתוּב, רַנְּנוּ צַדִּיקִים בַּיְיָ, לַיְשָׁרִים נָאוָה תְהִלָּה. בְּפִי יְשָׁרִים תִּתְהַלָּל. וּבְדִבְרֵי צַדִּיקִים תִּתְבָּרַךְ. וּבִלְשׁוֹן חֲסִידִים תִּתְרוֹמָם. וּבְקֶרֶב קְדוֹשִׁים תִּתְקַדָּשׁ:

וּבְמַקְהֲלוֹת רִבְבוֹת עַמְּךָ בֵּית יִשְׂרָאֵל, בְּרִנָּה יִתְפָּאֵר שִׁמְךָ מַלְכֵּנוּ, בְּכָל דּוֹר וָדוֹר, שֶׁכֵּן חוֹבַת כָּל הַיְצוּרִים, לְפָנֶיךָ יְיָ אֱלֹהֵינוּ, וֵאלֹהֵי אֲבוֹתֵינוּ, לְהוֹדוֹת לְהַלֵּל לְשַׁבֵּחַ לְפָאֵר לְרוֹמֵם לְהַדֵּר לְבָרֵךְ לְעַלֵּה וּלְקַלֵּס, עַל כָּל דִּבְרֵי שִׁירוֹת וְתִשְׁבְּחוֹת דָּוִד בֶּן יִשַׁי עַבְדְּךָ מְשִׁיחֶךָ:

to thank You sufficiently Hashem our God and God of our fathers, and bless Your Name, for even one of the thousands upon thousands and myriads upon myriads of favors You performed for our fathers and us: You freed us from Egypt, Hashem our God, and redeemed us from the house of bondage. You nourished us in famine and supported us in abundance. From the sword You saved us and You let us escape the plague; and You spared us from serious and lasting illnesses. Until now Your mercy has helped us, and Your kindness has not forsaken us. Do not abandon us, Hashem our God, for eternity. Therefore, the limbs which You have placed within us, the spirit and soul which You have breathed into our nostrils, and the tongue which You have placed in our mouth, shall all thank and bless, praise and glorify, exalt and esteem, sanctify and acclaim Your Name, our King. For every mouth shall offer thanks to You; every tongue shall vow allegiance to You; every knee shall bend to You; and all who stand erect shall bow before You. All hearts shall revere You, and men's inner beings shall sing (praises) to Your Name, as it is written: "all my bones shall say: Hashem, who is like You? You save the poor man from one that is stronger, the poor and needy from one who would rob him." Who may be likened to You? Who is equal to You? Who can be compared to You? Great, mighty and awesome God, supreme God, Master of heaven and earth. Let us praise, acclaim and glorify You and bless Your holy Name, as it says: A Psalm of David: "My soul should bless Hashem and my entire inner being should bless His holy Name."

God in Your mighty acts of power, great in the honor of Your Name, powerful forever and awesome for Your awe-inspiring acts, King seated upon a high and lofty throne!

He Who abides forever, exalted and holy is His Name. And it is written: "Rejoice in Hashem, you righteous; for the upright it is pleasant to give praise." By the mouth of the upright You shall be praised; By the words of the righteous You shall be blessed; By the tongue of the pious You shall be exalted; And in the midst of the holy You shall be sanctified.

In the assemblies of the myriads of Your people, the House of Yisrael, with song shall Your Name, our King, be glorified in every generation. For it is the duty of all creatures before You, Hashem, our God and God of our fathers to thank, praise, laud, extol, exalt, adore, and bless, elevate and sing praises; even beyond the songs and praises of David the son of Yishai, Your anointed servant.

יִשְׁתַּבַּח שִׁמְךָ לָעַד מַלְכֵּנוּ, הָאֵל הַמֶּלֶךְ הַגָּדוֹל וְהַקָּדוֹשׁ בַּשָּׁמַיִם וּבָאָרֶץ.

כִּי לְךָ נָאֶה, יְיָ אֱלֹהֵינוּ וֵאלֹהֵי אֲבוֹתֵינוּ: שִׁיר וּשְׁבָחָה, הַלֵּל וְזִמְרָה, עֹז וּמֶמְשָׁלָה, נֶצַח, גְּדֻלָּה וּגְבוּרָה, תְּהִלָּה וְתִפְאֶרֶת, קְדֻשָּׁה וּמַלְכוּת. בְּרָכוֹת וְהוֹדָאוֹת מֵעַתָּה וְעַד עוֹלָם. בָּרוּךְ אַתָּה יְיָ אֵל מֶלֶךְ גָּדוֹל בַּתִּשְׁבָּחוֹת אֵל הַהוֹדָאוֹת אֲדוֹן הַנִּפְלָאוֹת הַבּוֹחֵר בְּשִׁירֵי זִמְרָה מֶלֶךְ אֵל חֵי הָעוֹלָמִים.

שׁוֹתִים כּוֹס רְבִיעִית וּמְבָרְכִים בְּרָכָה אַחֲרוֹנָה

בָּרוּךְ אַתָּה יְיָ, אֱלֹהֵינוּ מֶלֶךְ הָעוֹלָם, בּוֹרֵא פְּרִי הַגָּפֶן:

בָּרוּךְ אַתָּה יְיָ אֱלֹהֵינוּ מֶלֶךְ הָעוֹלָם עַל הַגֶּפֶן וְעַל פְּרִי הַגֶּפֶן. וְעַל תְּנוּבַת הַשָּׂדֶה, וְעַל אֶרֶץ חֶמְדָּה טוֹבָה וּרְחָבָה, שֶׁרָצִיתָ וְהִנְחַלְתָּ לַאֲבוֹתֵינוּ, לֶאֱכוֹל מִפִּרְיָהּ וְלִשְׂבּוֹעַ מִטּוּבָהּ. רַחֵם נָא יְיָ אֱלֹהֵינוּ עַל יִשְׂרָאֵל עַמֶּךָ, וְעַל יְרוּשָׁלַיִם עִירֶךָ, וְעַל צִיּוֹן מִשְׁכַּן כְּבוֹדֶךָ, וְעַל מִזְבְּחֶךָ וְעַל הֵיכָלֶךָ. וּבְנֵה יְרוּשָׁלַיִם עִיר הַקֹּדֶשׁ בִּמְהֵרָה בְיָמֵינוּ, וְהַעֲלֵנוּ לְתוֹכָהּ, וְשַׂמְּחֵנוּ בְּבִנְיָנָהּ וְנֹאכַל מִפִּרְיָהּ וְנִשְׂבַּע מִטּוּבָהּ, וּנְבָרֶכְךָ עָלֶיהָ בִּקְדֻשָּׁה וּבְטָהֳרָה (בְּשַׁבָּת וּרְצֵה וְהַחֲלִיצֵנוּ בְּיוֹם הַשַּׁבָּת הַזֶּה.) וְשַׂמְּחֵנוּ בְּיוֹם חַג הַמַּצּוֹת הַזֶּה. כִּי אַתָּה יְיָ טוֹב וּמֵטִיב לַכֹּל, וְנוֹדֶה לְךָ עַל הָאָרֶץ וְעַל פְּרִי הַגָּפֶן. בָּרוּךְ אַתָּה יְיָ, עַל הָאָרֶץ וְעַל פְּרִי הַגָּפֶן:

ℤ נִרְצָה ℤ

חֲסַל סִדּוּר פֶּסַח כְּהִלְכָתוֹ, כְּכָל מִשְׁפָּטוֹ וְחֻקָּתוֹ. כַּאֲשֶׁר זָכִינוּ לְסַדֵּר אוֹתוֹ, כֵּן נִזְכֶּה לַעֲשׂוֹתוֹ. זָךְ שׁוֹכֵן מְעוֹנָה, קוֹמֵם קְהַל עֲדַת מִי מָנָה. בְּקָרוֹב נַהֵל נִטְעֵי כַנָּה, פְּדוּיִם לְצִיּוֹן בְּרִנָּה.

לְשָׁנָה הַבָּאָה בִּירוּשָׁלָיִם:

Praise be Your Name forever, our King, the God and King Who is great and holy in heaven and on earth; for to You, Hashem our God, it is fitting to render song and praise, *hallel* and music, power and dominion, victory, glory and might, praise and beauty, holiness and sovereignty, blessings and thanks, from now and forever. Blessed are You, Hashem, God, King, great in praises, God of thanksgivings, Master of wonders, Who prefers songs of praise, King, God, the Life of all worlds.

The fourth cup

Blessed are You, Hashem our God, King of the universe, Who creates the fruit of the vine.

Blessed, are You, Hashem our God, King of the universe, for the vine and its fruit, and for the produce of the field, for the beautiful, good and spacious land which You wanted to give to our fathers as a heritage, to eat of its fruit and to be replete with its goodness. Have mercy, please, Hashem our God, on Yisrael Your people, on Jerusalem Your city, on Zion the abode of Your glory, on Your altar and Your *Bais Hamikdash*. Rebuild Jerusalem, the holy city, speedily in our days. Bring us up there and cheer us with its restoration; may we eat of its fruit and be satisfied with its goodness; and may we bless You for it in holiness and purity. (*On Sabbath add:* Favor us and strengthen us on this Sabbath day) and grant us happiness on this Feast of Matzos; for You, Hashem, are good and beneficent to all, and we thank You for the land and the fruit of the vine. Blessed are You, Hashem for the land and the fruit of the vine.

❧ Nirtzah ☙

Acceptance: The Seder is accepted by God

The Seder now concludes according to *Halachah,* complete in all its laws and ordinances. Just as we were privileged to arrange it (tonight), so may we merit to perform it (again). Pure One Who dwells in the heights above, raise up the countless congregation, soon guide the seedlings of Your plants (Yisrael), redeemed to Zion with song.

Next year in Jerusalem

וּבְכֵן "וַיְהִי בַּחֲצִי הַלַּיְלָה".

אָז רוֹב נִסִּים הִפְלֵאתָ בַּלַּיְלָה, בְּרֹאשׁ אַשְׁמוֹרוֹת זֶה הַלַּיְלָה, גֵּר צֶדֶק נִצַּחְתּוֹ כְּנֶחֱלַק לוֹ לַיְלָה, וַיְהִי בַּחֲצִי הַלַּיְלָה.

דַּנְתָּ מֶלֶךְ גְּרָר בַּחֲלוֹם הַלַּיְלָה, הִפְחַדְתָּ אֲרַמִּי בְּאֶמֶשׁ לַיְלָה, וַיָּשַׂר יִשְׂרָאֵל לְמַלְאָךְ וַיּוּכַל לוֹ לַיְלָה, וַיְהִי בַּחֲצִי הַלַּיְלָה.

זֶרַע בְּכוֹרֵי פַתְרוֹס מָחַצְתָּ בַּחֲצִי הַלַּיְלָה, חֵילָם לֹא מָצְאוּ בְּקוּמָם בַּלַּיְלָה, טִיסַת נְגִיד חֲרֹשֶׁת סִלִּיתָ בְּכוֹכְבֵי לַיְלָה, וַיְהִי בַּחֲצִי הַלַּיְלָה.

יָעַץ מְחָרֵף לְנוֹפֵף אִוּוּי, הוֹבַשְׁתָּ פְגָרָיו בַּלַּיְלָה, כָּרַע בֵּל וּמַצָּבוֹ בְּאִישׁוֹן לַיְלָה, לְאִישׁ חֲמוּדוֹת נִגְלָה רָז חֲזוֹת לַיְלָה, וַיְהִי בַּחֲצִי הַלַּיְלָה.

מִשְׁתַּכֵּר בִּכְלֵי קֹדֶשׁ נֶהֱרַג בּוֹ בַּלַּיְלָה, נוֹשַׁע מִבּוֹר אֲרָיוֹת פּוֹתֵר בְּעִתּוּתֵי לַיְלָה, שִׂנְאָה נָטַר אֲגָגִי וְכָתַב סְפָרִים בַּלַּיְלָה, וַיְהִי בַּחֲצִי הַלַּיְלָה.

עוֹרַרְתָּ נִצְחֲךָ עָלָיו בְּנֶדֶד שְׁנַת לַיְלָה, פּוּרָה תִדְרוֹךְ לְשׁוֹמֵר מַה מִּלַּיְלָה, צָרַח כַּשֹּׁמֵר וְשָׂח אָתָא בֹקֶר וְגַם לַיְלָה, וַיְהִי בַּחֲצִי הַלַּיְלָה.

קָרֵב יוֹם אֲשֶׁר הוּא לֹא יוֹם וְלֹא לַיְלָה, רָם הוֹדַע כִּי לְךָ הַיּוֹם אַף לְךָ הַלַּיְלָה, שׁוֹמְרִים הַפְקֵד לְעִירְךָ כָּל הַיּוֹם וְכָל הַלַּיְלָה, תָּאִיר כְּאוֹר יוֹם חֶשְׁכַּת לַיְלָה, וַיְהִי בַּחֲצִי הַלַּיְלָה:

בליל סדר שני

וּבְכֵן "וַאֲמַרְתֶּם זֶבַח פֶּסַח"

אֹמֶץ גְּבוּרוֹתֶיךָ הִפְלֵאתָ בַּפֶּסַח, בְּרֹאשׁ כָּל מוֹעֲדוֹת נִשֵּׂאתָ פֶּסַח, גִּלִּיתָ לְאֶזְרָחִי חֲצוֹת לֵיל פֶּסַח, וַאֲמַרְתֶּם זֶבַח פֶּסַח.

It came to pass at midnight

You did perform then a multitude of wonders at night: In the early watches of this night; The righteous convert (Avraham) did You cause to triumph by dividing for him the night; It came to pass at midnight.

Grar's king (Avimelech), You judged in a dream by night; You did frighten the Aramean (Lavan) in the dark of night; Yisrael (Yaakov) fought with an angel and overcame him by night; It came to pass at midnight.

Egypt's firstborn did You crush at midnight; Their strength they found not when they rose at night. The army of the prince of Charoshes (Sisera) did You sweep away with the stars of the night; It came to pass at midnight.

The blasphemer (Sancheriv) planned to attack Jerusalem, but You shriveled his corpses by night; Bel (Babylon's idol) fell with its pedestal in the dark of night; To the pleasant man (Daniel) was revealed the secrets of the visions of the night; It came to pass at midnight.

He (Belshazzar), who became intoxicated while using the holy vessels (*Bais Hamikdash's*), was killed that same night; He (Daniel) was saved from the lion's den and interpreted the terrifying visions of night; The Agagite (Haman) who bore a grudge and wrote letters in the night; It came to pass at midnight.

Your triumph over him (Haman) began when You induced the king's insomnia; Trample the winepress and aid those who ask the watchman; "What of the night?" He will shout like a watchman and respond: "Morning comes after night"; It came to pass at midnight.

Hasten the day (of *Moshiach*) which is not really day or night; Exalted One, proclaim that Yours are day and night; Set guards about Your city all day and all night; Brighten as day the darkness of the night; It came to pass at midnight.

On the second night, recite:
And you shall say: It is the Pesach sacrifice

Your wondrous powers did You display on Pesach; Chief of all festivals did You elevate Pesach; You did reveal to the Ezrachi (Avraham) the future midnight of Pesach; And you shall say: It is the Pesach sacrifice.

דְּלָתָיו דָּפַקְתָּ כְּחֹם הַיּוֹם בַּפֶּסַח, הִסְעִיד נוֹצְצִים עֻגוֹת מַצּוֹת בַּפֶּסַח, וְאֶל הַבָּקָר רָץ זֵכֶר לְשׁוֹר עֵרֶךְ פֶּסַח, וַאֲמַרְתֶּם זֶבַח פֶּסַח.

זֹעֲמוּ סְדוֹמִים וְלֹהֲטוּ בָּאֵשׁ בַּפֶּסַח, חֻלַּץ לוֹט מֵהֶם, וּמַצּוֹת אָפָה בְּקֵץ פֶּסַח, טִאטֵאתָ אַדְמַת מֹף וְנֹף בְּעָבְרְךָ בַּפֶּסַח, וַאֲמַרְתֶּם זֶבַח פֶּסַח.

יָהּ, רֹאשׁ כָּל אוֹן מָחַצְתָּ בְּלֵיל שִׁמּוּר פֶּסַח, כַּבִּיר, עַל בֵּן בְּכוֹר פָּסַחְתָּ בְּדַם פֶּסַח, לְבִלְתִּי תֵּת מַשְׁחִית לָבֹא בִּפְתָחַי בַּפֶּסַח, וַאֲמַרְתֶּם זֶבַח פֶּסַח.

מְסֻגֶּרֶת סֻגָּרָה בְּעִתּוֹתֵי פֶּסַח, נִשְׁמְדָה מִדְיָן בִּצְלִיל שְׂעוֹרֵי עֹמֶר פֶּסַח, שֹׂרְפוּ מִשְׁמַנֵּי פּוּל וְלוּד בִּיקַד יְקוֹד פֶּסַח, וַאֲמַרְתֶּם זֶבַח פֶּסַח.

עוֹד הַיּוֹם בְּנֹב לַעֲמוֹד, עַד גָּעָה עוֹנַת פֶּסַח, פַּס יָד כָּתְבָה לְקַעֲקֵעַ צוּל בַּפֶּסַח, צָפֹה הַצָּפִית עָרוֹךְ הַשֻּׁלְחָן, בַּפֶּסַח, וַאֲמַרְתֶּם זֶבַח פֶּסַח.

קָהָל כִּנְּסָה הֲדַסָּה צוֹם לְשַׁלֵּשׁ בַּפֶּסַח, רֹאשׁ מִבֵּית רָשָׁע מָחַצְתָּ בְּעֵץ חֲמִשִּׁים בַּפֶּסַח, שְׁתֵּי אֵלֶּה רֶגַע, תָּבִיא לְעוּצִית בַּפֶּסַח, תָּעֹז יָדְךָ וְתָרוּם יְמִינֶךָ, כְּלֵיל הִתְקַדֶּשׁ חַג פֶּסַח, וַאֲמַרְתֶּם זֶבַח פֶּסַח.

כִּי לוֹ נָאֶה, כִּי לוֹ יָאֶה.

אַדִּיר בִּמְלוּכָה, בָּחוּר כַּהֲלָכָה, גְּדוּדָיו יֹאמְרוּ לוֹ: לְךָ וּלְךָ, לְךָ כִּי לְךָ, לְךָ אַף לְךָ, לְךָ יְיָ הַמַּמְלָכָה. כִּי לוֹ נָאֶה, כִּי לוֹ יָאֶה.

דָּגוּל בִּמְלוּכָה, הָדוּר כַּהֲלָכָה, וָתִיקָיו יֹאמְרוּ לוֹ: לְךָ וּלְךָ, לְךָ כִּי לְךָ, לְךָ אַף לְךָ, לְךָ יְיָ הַמַּמְלָכָה. כִּי לוֹ נָאֶה, כִּי לוֹ יָאֶה.

זַכַּאי בִּמְלוּכָה, חָסִין כַּהֲלָכָה, טַפְסְרָיו יֹאמְרוּ לוֹ: לְךָ וּלְךָ, לְךָ כִּי לְךָ, לְךָ אַף לְךָ, לְךָ יְיָ הַמַּמְלָכָה. כִּי לוֹ נָאֶה, כִּי לוֹ יָאֶה.

His door did You knock in the heat of day on Pesach; With matzos he fed angels on Pesach; To the herd he ran as a symbol of the sacrificial animal of Pesach; And you shall say: It is the Pesach sacrifice.

The men of Sodom angered (God) and were burned in wrath on Pesach; Lot was rescued from them, he baked matzos at the time of Pesach; You swept the land of Moph and Noph (in Egypt) when You passed through on Pesach; And you shall say: It is the Pesach sacrifice.

God, every firstborn of On (in Egypt) You did crush on the guarded night of Pesach; But Almighty, Your firstborn You did pass over in the merit of the blood of the Pesach; So that the Destroyer was not permitted to enter my (Yisrael's) doors on Pesach; And you shall say: It is the Pesach sacrifice.

The tightly closed city of Jericho was besieged on Pesach; Midian was destroyed with a barley-cake from the Omer of Pesach; Pul and Lud's (Assyria) mighty armies were consumed by a great fire on Pesach; And you shall say: It is the Pesach sacrifice.

He (Sancheriv) would have held his ground at Nov but for the season of Pesach; A hand inscribed Zul's (Babylon) destruction on Pesach; when the guard was posted and the festive table was set on Pesach; And you shall say: It is the Pesach sacrifice.

Hadassah (Esther) gathered a congregation for a three-day fast on Pesach; You did hang the head of the evil family (Haman) on a fifty cubit gallows on Pesach; Doubly, will You punish in an instant Utsis (Edom) on Pesach; Let Your hand be strong and Your right arm elevated as on the night when You sanctified the festival of Pesach; And you shall say: It is the Pesach sacrifice.

To Him praises are due; to Him it is befitting!

Powerful in kingship, truly chosen, His troops (of angels) say to Him: "Yours only Yours, Yours for it's Yours; Yours surely Yours; Yours Hashem, is the Kingdom."
To Him praises are due, to Him it is befitting!

Prominent in kingship, truly glorious, His faithful say to Him: "Yours only Yours, Yours for it's Yours; Yours surely Yours; Yours Hashem, is the Kingdom."
To Him praises are due, to Him it is befitting!

Worthy of kingship, truly strong, His angels say to Him: "Yours only Yours, Yours for it's Yours; Yours surely Yours; Yours Hashem, is the Kingdom."
To Him praises are due, to Him it is befitting!

יָחִיד בִּמְלוּכָה, כַּבִּיר כַּהֲלָכָה, לִמּוּדָיו יֹאמְרוּ לוֹ: לְךָ וּלְךָ, לְךָ כִּי לְךָ, לְךָ אַף לְךָ, לְךָ יְיָ הַמַּמְלָכָה. כִּי לוֹ נָאֶה, כִּי לוֹ יָאֶה.

מוֹשֵׁל בִּמְלוּכָה, נוֹרָא כַּהֲלָכָה, סְבִיבָיו יֹאמְרוּ לוֹ: לְךָ וּלְךָ, לְךָ כִּי לְךָ, לְךָ אַף לְךָ, לְךָ יְיָ הַמַּמְלָכָה. כִּי לוֹ נָאֶה, כִּי לוֹ יָאֶה.

עָנָו בִּמְלוּכָה, פּוֹדֶה כַּהֲלָכָה, צַדִּיקָיו יֹאמְרוּ לוֹ: לְךָ וּלְךָ, לְךָ כִּי לְךָ, לְךָ אַף לְךָ, לְךָ יְיָ הַמַּמְלָכָה. כִּי לוֹ נָאֶה, כִּי לוֹ יָאֶה.

קָדוֹשׁ בִּמְלוּכָה, רַחוּם כַּהֲלָכָה, שִׁנְאַנָּיו יֹאמְרוּ לוֹ: לְךָ וּלְךָ, לְךָ כִּי לְךָ, לְךָ אַף לְךָ, לְךָ יְיָ הַמַּמְלָכָה. כִּי לוֹ נָאֶה, כִּי לוֹ יָאֶה.

תַּקִּיף בִּמְלוּכָה, תּוֹמֵךְ כַּהֲלָכָה, תְּמִימָיו יֹאמְרוּ לוֹ: לְךָ וּלְךָ, לְךָ כִּי לְךָ, לְךָ אַף לְךָ, לְךָ יְיָ הַמַּמְלָכָה. כִּי לוֹ נָאֶה, כִּי לוֹ יָאֶה.

אַדִּיר הוּא, יִבְנֶה בֵיתוֹ בְּקָרוֹב, בִּמְהֵרָה בִּמְהֵרָה, בְּיָמֵינוּ בְּקָרוֹב. אֵל בְּנֵה, אֵל בְּנֵה, בְּנֵה בֵיתְךָ בְּקָרוֹב.

בָּחוּר הוּא, גָּדוֹל הוּא, דָּגוּל הוּא, יִבְנֶה בֵיתוֹ בְּקָרוֹב, בִּמְהֵרָה בִּמְהֵרָה, בְּיָמֵינוּ בְּקָרוֹב. אֵל בְּנֵה, אֵל בְּנֵה, בְּנֵה בֵיתְךָ בְּקָרוֹב.

הָדוּר הוּא, וָתִיק הוּא, זַכַּאי הוּא, יִבְנֶה בֵיתוֹ בְּקָרוֹב, בִּמְהֵרָה בִּמְהֵרָה, בְּיָמֵינוּ בְּקָרוֹב. אֵל בְּנֵה, אֵל בְּנֵה, בְּנֵה בֵיתְךָ בְּקָרוֹב.

חָסִיד הוּא, טָהוֹר הוּא, יָחִיד הוּא, יִבְנֶה בֵיתוֹ בְּקָרוֹב, בִּמְהֵרָה בִּמְהֵרָה, בְּיָמֵינוּ בְּקָרוֹב. אֵל בְּנֵה, אֵל בְּנֵה, בְּנֵה בֵיתְךָ בְּקָרוֹב.

כַּבִּיר הוּא, לָמוּד הוּא, מֶלֶךְ הוּא, יִבְנֶה בֵיתוֹ בְּקָרוֹב, בִּמְהֵרָה בִּמְהֵרָה, בְּיָמֵינוּ בְּקָרוֹב. אֵל בְּנֵה, אֵל בְּנֵה, בְּנֵה בֵיתְךָ בְּקָרוֹב.

נוֹרָא הוּא, סַגִּיב הוּא, עִזּוּז הוּא, יִבְנֶה בֵיתוֹ בְּקָרוֹב, בִּמְהֵרָה בִּמְהֵרָה, בְּיָמֵינוּ בְּקָרוֹב. אֵל בְּנֵה, אֵל בְּנֵה, בְּנֵה בֵיתְךָ בְּקָרוֹב.

Alone in kingship, truly great, His scholars say to Him:
"Yours only Yours, Yours for it's Yours; Yours surely Yours;
Yours Hashem, is the Kingdom."
To Him praises are due, to Him it is befitting!

Commanding in kingship, truly awesome, His surrounding (angels)
say to Him: "Yours only Yours, Yours for it's Yours; Yours surely
Yours; Yours Hashem, is the Kingdom."
To Him praises are due, to Him it is befitting!

Humble in kingship, truly the Redeemer, His righteous say to Him:
"Yours only Yours, Yours for it's Yours; Yours surely Yours;
Yours Hashem, is the Kingdom."
To Him praises are due, to Him it is befitting!

Holy in kingship, truly merciful, His troops of angels say to Him:
"Yours only Yours, Yours for it's Yours; Yours surely Yours;
Yours Hashem, is the Kingdom."
To Him praises are due, to Him it is befitting!

Indomitable in kingship, truly sustaining, His innocent say to Him:
"Yours only Yours, Yours for it's Yours; Yours surely Yours;
Yours Hashem, is the Kingdom."
To Him praises are due, to Him it is befitting!

He is powerful, May He rebuild His *Bais Hamikdash* soon. Soon, very soon, in our days, soon, God, rebuild Your *Bais Hamikdash* speedily.

He is chosen, He is great, He is exalted; May He rebuild His *Bais Hamikdash* soon. Soon, very soon, in our days, soon, God, rebuild Your *Bais Hamikdash* speedily.

He is glorious, He is pure, He is worthy; May He rebuild His *Bais Hamikdash* soon. Soon, very soon, in our days, soon, God, rebuild Your *Bais Hamikdash* speedily.

He is pious, He is pure, He is unique; May He rebuild His *Bais Hamikdash* soon. Soon, very soon, in our days, soon, God, rebuild Your *Bais Hamikdash* speedily.

He is powerful, He is wise, He is King; May He rebuild His *Bais Hamikdash* soon. Soon, very soon, in our days, soon, God, rebuild Your *Bais Hamikdash* speedily.

He is awesome, He is mighty, He is strong; May He rebuild His *Bais Hamikdash* soon. Soon, very soon, in our days, soon, God, rebuild Your *Bais Hamikdash* speedily.

פּוֹדֶה הוּא, צַדִּיק הוּא, קָדוֹשׁ הוּא, יִבְנֶה בֵיתוֹ בְּקָרוֹב, בִּמְהֵרָה בִּמְהֵרָה, בְּיָמֵינוּ בְּקָרוֹב. אֵל בְּנֵה, אֵל בְּנֵה, בְּנֵה בֵיתְךָ בְּקָרוֹב.

רַחוּם הוּא, שַׁדַּי הוּא, תַּקִּיף הוּא, יִבְנֶה בֵיתוֹ בְּקָרוֹב, בִּמְהֵרָה בִּמְהֵרָה, בְּיָמֵינוּ בְּקָרוֹב. אֵל בְּנֵה, אֵל בְּנֵה, בְּנֵה בֵיתְךָ בְּקָרוֹב.

אֶחָד מִי יוֹדֵעַ? אֶחָד אֲנִי יוֹדֵעַ: אֶחָד אֱלֹהֵינוּ שֶׁבַּשָּׁמַיִם וּבָאָרֶץ.

שְׁנַיִם מִי יוֹדֵעַ? שְׁנַיִם אֲנִי יוֹדֵעַ: שְׁנֵי לֻחוֹת הַבְּרִית, אֶחָד אֱלֹהֵינוּ שֶׁבַּשָּׁמַיִם וּבָאָרֶץ.

שְׁלֹשָׁה מִי יוֹדֵעַ? שְׁלֹשָׁה אֲנִי יוֹדֵעַ: שְׁלֹשָׁה אָבוֹת, שְׁנֵי לֻחוֹת הַבְּרִית, אֶחָד אֱלֹהֵינוּ שֶׁבַּשָּׁמַיִם וּבָאָרֶץ.

אַרְבַּע מִי יוֹדֵעַ? אַרְבַּע אֲנִי יוֹדֵעַ: אַרְבַּע אִמָּהוֹת, שְׁלֹשָׁה אָבוֹת, שְׁנֵי לֻחוֹת הַבְּרִית, אֶחָד אֱלֹהֵינוּ שֶׁבַּשָּׁמַיִם וּבָאָרֶץ.

חֲמִשָּׁה מִי יוֹדֵעַ? חֲמִשָּׁה אֲנִי יוֹדֵעַ: חֲמִשָּׁה חוּמְשֵׁי תוֹרָה, אַרְבַּע אִמָּהוֹת, שְׁלֹשָׁה אָבוֹת, שְׁנֵי לֻחוֹת הַבְּרִית, אֶחָד אֱלֹהֵינוּ שֶׁבַּשָּׁמַיִם וּבָאָרֶץ.

שִׁשָּׁה מִי יוֹדֵעַ? שִׁשָּׁה אֲנִי יוֹדֵעַ: שִׁשָּׁה סִדְרֵי מִשְׁנָה, חֲמִשָּׁה חוּמְשֵׁי תוֹרָה, אַרְבַּע אִמָּהוֹת, שְׁלֹשָׁה אָבוֹת, שְׁנֵי לֻחוֹת הַבְּרִית, אֶחָד אֱלֹהֵינוּ שֶׁבַּשָּׁמַיִם וּבָאָרֶץ.

שִׁבְעָה מִי יוֹדֵעַ? שִׁבְעָה אֲנִי יוֹדֵעַ: שִׁבְעָה יְמֵי שַׁבַּתָּא, שִׁשָּׁה סִדְרֵי מִשְׁנָה, חֲמִשָּׁה חוּמְשֵׁי תוֹרָה, אַרְבַּע אִמָּהוֹת, שְׁלֹשָׁה אָבוֹת, שְׁנֵי לֻחוֹת הַבְּרִית, אֶחָד אֱלֹהֵינוּ שֶׁבַּשָּׁמַיִם וּבָאָרֶץ.

שְׁמוֹנָה מִי יוֹדֵעַ? שְׁמוֹנָה אֲנִי יוֹדֵעַ: שְׁמוֹנָה יְמֵי מִילָה, שִׁבְעָה יְמֵי שַׁבַּתָּא, שִׁשָּׁה סִדְרֵי מִשְׁנָה, חֲמִשָּׁה חוּמְשֵׁי תוֹרָה, אַרְבַּע אִמָּהוֹת, שְׁלֹשָׁה אָבוֹת, שְׁנֵי לֻחוֹת הַבְּרִית, אֶחָד אֱלֹהֵינוּ שֶׁבַּשָּׁמַיִם וּבָאָרֶץ.

He is the Redeemer, He is righteous, He is holy; May He rebuild His *Bais Hamikdash* soon. Soon, very soon, in our days, soon, God, rebuild Your *Bais Hamikdash* speedily.

He is merciful, He is Almighty, He is indomitable; May He rebuild His *Bais Hamikdash* very soon. Soon, very soon, in our days, soon, God, rebuild Your *Bais Hamikdash* speedily.

Who knows one?

Who knows *one*? I know *one*! One is our God in heaven and on earth.

Who knows *two*? I know *two*! Two are the Tablets of the Covenant; One is our God in heaven and on earth.

Who knows *three*? I know *three*! Three are Patriarchs; Two are the Tablets of the Covenant; One is our God in heaven and on earth.

Who knows *four*? I know *four*! Four are the Matriarchs; Three are the Patriarchs; Two are the Tablets of the Covenant; One is our God in heaven and on earth.

Who knows *five*? I know *five*! Five are the books of the Torah; Four are the Matriarchs; Three are the Patriarchs; Two are the Tablets of the Covenant; One is our God in heaven and on earth.

Who knows *six*? I know *six*! Six are the Orders of the Mishnah; Five are the books of the Torah; Four are the Matriarchs; Three are the Patriarchs ; Two are the Tablets of the Covenant; One is our God in heaven and on earth.

Who knows *seven*? I know *seven*! Seven are the days of the week; Six are the Orders of the Mishnah; Five are the books of the Torah; Four are the Matriarchs; Three are the Patriarchs; Two are the Tablets of the Covenant; One is our God in heaven and on earth.

Who knows *eight*? I know *eight*! Eight are the days to circumcision; Seven are the days of the week; Six are the Orders of the Mishnah; Five are the books of the Torah; Four are the Matriarchs; Three are the Patriarchs; Two are the Tablets of the Covenant; One is our God in heaven and on earth.

תִּשְׁעָה מִי יוֹדֵעַ? תִּשְׁעָה אֲנִי יוֹדֵעַ: תִּשְׁעָה יַרְחֵי לֵדָה, שְׁמוֹנָה יְמֵי מִילָה, שִׁבְעָה יְמֵי שַׁבַּתָּא, שִׁשָּׁה סִדְרֵי מִשְׁנָה, חֲמִשָּׁה חוּמְשֵׁי תוֹרָה, אַרְבַּע אִמָּהוֹת, שְׁלֹשָׁה אָבוֹת, שְׁנֵי לֻחוֹת הַבְּרִית, אֶחָד אֱלֹהֵינוּ שֶׁבַּשָּׁמַיִם וּבָאָרֶץ.

עֲשָׂרָה מִי יוֹדֵעַ? עֲשָׂרָה אֲנִי יוֹדֵעַ: עֲשָׂרָה דִבְּרַיָּא, תִּשְׁעָה יַרְחֵי לֵדָה, שְׁמוֹנָה יְמֵי מִילָה, שִׁבְעָה יְמֵי שַׁבַּתָּא, שִׁשָּׁה סִדְרֵי מִשְׁנָה, חֲמִשָּׁה חוּמְשֵׁי תוֹרָה, אַרְבַּע אִמָּהוֹת, שְׁלֹשָׁה אָבוֹת, שְׁנֵי לֻחוֹת הַבְּרִית, אֶחָד אֱלֹהֵינוּ שֶׁבַּשָּׁמַיִם וּבָאָרֶץ.

אַחַד עָשָׂר מִי יוֹדֵעַ? אַחַד עָשָׂר אֲנִי יוֹדֵעַ: אַחַד עָשָׂר כּוֹכְבַיָּא, עֲשָׂרָה דִבְּרַיָּא, תִּשְׁעָה יַרְחֵי לֵדָה, שְׁמוֹנָה יְמֵי מִילָה, שִׁבְעָה יְמֵי שַׁבַּתָּא, שִׁשָּׁה סִדְרֵי מִשְׁנָה, חֲמִשָּׁה חוּמְשֵׁי תוֹרָה, אַרְבַּע אִמָּהוֹת, שְׁלֹשָׁה אָבוֹת, שְׁנֵי לֻחוֹת הַבְּרִית, אֶחָד אֱלֹהֵינוּ שֶׁבַּשָּׁמַיִם וּבָאָרֶץ.

שְׁנֵים עָשָׂר מִי יוֹדֵעַ? שְׁנֵים עָשָׂר אֲנִי יוֹדֵעַ: שְׁנֵים עָשָׂר שִׁבְטַיָּא, אַחַד עָשָׂר כּוֹכְבַיָּא, עֲשָׂרָה דִבְּרַיָּא, תִּשְׁעָה יַרְחֵי לֵדָה, שְׁמוֹנָה יְמֵי מִילָה, שִׁבְעָה יְמֵי שַׁבַּתָּא, שִׁשָּׁה סִדְרֵי מִשְׁנָה, חֲמִשָּׁה חוּמְשֵׁי תוֹרָה, אַרְבַּע אִמָּהוֹת, שְׁלֹשָׁה אָבוֹת, שְׁנֵי לֻחוֹת הַבְּרִית, אֶחָד אֱלֹהֵינוּ שֶׁבַּשָּׁמַיִם וּבָאָרֶץ.

שְׁלֹשָׁה עָשָׂר מִי יוֹדֵעַ? שְׁלֹשָׁה עָשָׂר אֲנִי יוֹדֵעַ: שְׁלֹשָׁה עָשָׂר מִדַּיָּא, שְׁנֵים עָשָׂר שִׁבְטַיָּא, אַחַד עָשָׂר כּוֹכְבַיָּא, עֲשָׂרָה דִבְּרַיָּא, תִּשְׁעָה יַרְחֵי לֵדָה, שְׁמוֹנָה יְמֵי מִילָה, שִׁבְעָה יְמֵי שַׁבַּתָּא, שִׁשָּׁה סִדְרֵי מִשְׁנָה, חֲמִשָּׁה חוּמְשֵׁי תוֹרָה, אַרְבַּע אִמָּהוֹת, שְׁלֹשָׁה אָבוֹת, שְׁנֵי לֻחוֹת הַבְּרִית, אֶחָד אֱלֹהֵינוּ שֶׁבַּשָּׁמַיִם וּבָאָרֶץ.

Who knows *nine*? I know *nine*! Nine are the months to childbirth; Eight are the days to circumcision; Seven are the days of the week; Six are the Orders of the Mishnah; Five are the books of the Torah; Four are the Matriarchs; Three are the Patriarchs ; Two are the Tablets of the Covenant; One is our God in heaven and on earth.

Who knows *ten*? I know *ten*! Ten are the Ten Commandments; Nine are the months to childbirth; Eight are the days to circumcision; Seven are the days of the week; Six are the Orders of the Mishnah; Five are the books of the Torah; Four are the Matriarchs; Three are the Patriarchs; Two are the Tablets of the Covenant; One is our God in heaven and on earth.

Who knows *eleven*? I know *eleven*! Eleven are the stars (in Joseph's dream); Ten are the Ten Commandments; Nine are the months to childbirth; Eight are the days to circumcision; Seven are the days of the week; Six are the Orders of the Mishnah; Five are the books of the Torah; Four are the Matriarchs; Three are the Patriarchs; Two are the Tablets of the Covenant; One is our God in heaven and on earth.

Who knows *twelve*? I know *twelve*! Twelve are the tribes (of Yisrael); Eleven are the stars (in Joseph's dream); Ten are the Ten Commandments; Nine are the months to childbirth; Eight are the days to circumcision; Seven are the days of the week; Six are the Orders of the Mishnah; Five are the books of the Torah; Four are the Matriarchs; Three are the Patriarchs; Two are the Tablets of the Covenant; One is our God in heaven and on earth.

Who knows *thirteen*? I know *thirteen*! Thirteen are the attributes of God; Twelve are the tribes (of Yisrael); Eleven are the stars (in Joseph's dream); Ten are the Ten Commandments; Nine are the months to childbirth; Eight are the days to circumcision; Seven are the days of the week; Six are the Orders of the Mishnah; Five are the books of the Torah; Four are Matriarchs; Three are the Patriarchs; Two are the Tablets of the Covenant; One is our God in heaven and on earth.

חַד גַּדְיָא

חַד גַּדְיָא, חַד גַּדְיָא דְּזַבִּין אַבָּא בִּתְרֵי זוּזֵי, חַד גַּדְיָא, חַד גַּדְיָא.

וְאָתָא שׁוּנְרָא, וְאָכְלָה לְגַדְיָא, דְּזַבִּין אַבָּא בִּתְרֵי זוּזֵי, חַד גַּדְיָא, חַד גַּדְיָא.

וְאָתָא כַלְבָּא, וְנָשַׁךְ לְשׁוּנְרָא, דְּאָכְלָה לְגַדְיָא, דְּזַבִּין אַבָּא בִּתְרֵי זוּזֵי, חַד גַּדְיָא, חַד גַּדְיָא.

וְאָתָא חוּטְרָא, וְהִכָּה לְכַלְבָּא, דְּנָשַׁךְ לְשׁוּנְרָא, דְּאָכְלָה לְגַדְיָא, דְּזַבִּין אַבָּא בִּתְרֵי זוּזֵי, חַד גַּדְיָא, חַד גַּדְיָא.

וְאָתָא נוּרָא, וְשָׂרַף לְחוּטְרָא, דְּהִכָּה לְכַלְבָּא, דְּנָשַׁךְ לְשׁוּנְרָא, דְּאָכְלָה לְגַדְיָא, דְּזַבִּין אַבָּא בִּתְרֵי זוּזֵי, חַד גַּדְיָא, חַד גַּדְיָא.

וְאָתָא מַיָּא, וְכָבָה לְנוּרָא, דְּשָׂרַף לְחוּטְרָא, דְּהִכָּה לְכַלְבָּא, דְּנָשַׁךְ לְשׁוּנְרָא, דְּאָכְלָה לְגַדְיָא, דְּזַבִּין אַבָּא בִּתְרֵי זוּזֵי, חַד גַּדְיָא, חַד גַּדְיָא.

וְאָתָא תוֹרָא, וְשָׁתָא לְמַיָּא, דְּכָבָה לְנוּרָא, דְּשָׂרַף לְחוּטְרָא, דְּהִכָּה לְכַלְבָּא, דְּנָשַׁךְ לְשׁוּנְרָא, דְּאָכְלָה לְגַדְיָא, דְּזַבִּין אַבָּא בִּתְרֵי זוּזֵי, חַד גַּדְיָא, חַד גַּדְיָא.

וְאָתָא הַשּׁוֹחֵט, וְשָׁחַט לְתוֹרָא, דְּשָׁתָא לְמַיָּא, דְּכָבָה לְנוּרָא, דְּשָׂרַף לְחוּטְרָא, דְּהִכָּה לְכַלְבָּא, דְּנָשַׁךְ לְשׁוּנְרָא, דְּאָכְלָה לְגַדְיָא, דְּזַבִּין אַבָּא בִּתְרֵי זוּזֵי, חַד גַּדְיָא, חַד גַּדְיָא.

וְאָתָא מַלְאַךְ הַמָּוֶת, וְשָׁחַט לְשׁוֹחֵט, דְּשָׁחַט לְתוֹרָא, דְּשָׁתָא לְמַיָּא, דְּכָבָה לְנוּרָא, דְּשָׂרַף לְחוּטְרָא, דְּהִכָּה לְכַלְבָּא, דְּנָשַׁךְ לְשׁוּנְרָא, דְּאָכְלָה לְגַדְיָא, דְּזַבִּין אַבָּא בִּתְרֵי זוּזֵי, חַד גַּדְיָא, חַד גַּדְיָא.

וְאָתָא הַקָּדוֹשׁ בָּרוּךְ הוּא, וְשָׁחַט לְמַלְאַךְ הַמָּוֶת, דְּשָׁחַט לְתוֹרָא, דְּשָׁתָא לְמַיָּא, דְּכָבָה לְנוּרָא, דְּשָׂרַף לְחוּטְרָא, דְּהִכָּה לְכַלְבָּא, דְּנָשַׁךְ לְשׁוּנְרָא, דְּאָכְלָה לְגַדְיָא, דְּזַבִּין אַבָּא בִּתְרֵי זוּזֵי, חַד גַּדְיָא, חַד גַּדְיָא.

One kid

One kid, one kid that father bought for two zuzim; One kid, one kid.

The cat came and ate the kid that father bought for two zuzim; One kid, one kid.

The dog came and bit the cat, that ate the kid that father bought for two zuzim; One kid, one kid.

The stick came, and beat the dog, that bit the cat, that ate the kid that father bought for two zuzim; One kid, one kid.

The fire came and burned the stick, that beat the dog, that bit the cat, that ate the kid that father bought for two zuzim; One kid, one kid.

The water came and quenched the fire, that burned the stick, that beat the dog, that bit the cat, that ate the kid that father bought for two zuzim; One kid, one kid.

The ox came and drank the water, that quenched the fire, that burned the stick, that beat the dog, that bit the cat, that ate the kid that father bought for two zuzim; One kid, one kid.

The slaughterer came and killed the ox, that drank the water, that quenched the fire, that burned the stick, that beat the dog, that bit the cat, that ate the kid that father bought for two zuzim; One kid, one kid.

The angel of death came and slew the slaughterer, that killed the ox, that drank the water, that quenched the fire, that burned the stick, that beat the dog, that bit the cat, that ate the kid that father bought for two zuzim; One kid, one kid.

The Holy One, Blessed is He, came and slew the angel of death, that slew the slaughterer, that killed the ox, that drank the water, that quenched the fire, that burned the stick, that beat the dog, that bit the cat, that ate the kid that father bought for two zuzim; One kid, one kid.